Starmont Reference Guide #12

A Bibliographic Chronicle of
ACE MYSTERY DOUBLES

DOUBLE TROUBLE

Sheldon Jaffery

Complete and
Unabridged

BORGO PRESS / WILDSIDE PRESS

www.wildsidepress.com

Contents

References

Albert, Walter. *Detective and Mystery Fiction: An International Bibliography of Secondary Sources.* First edition. Brownstone Books, Madison (1985).

Bourgeau, Art. *The Mystery Lover's Companion.* First edition. Crown Publishers, Inc,. New York. (1986).

Barzun, Jacques & Taylor, Wendell Hertig. *A Catalogue of Crime: Being A Reader's Guide to the Literature of Mystery, Detection & Related Genres.* First Edition. Harper & Row, New York (1971).

Cook, Michael. *Monthly Murders: A Checklist and Chronological Listing of Fiction in the Digest-Size Mystery Magazines in the United States and England.* First edition. Greenwood Press, Westport, IN (1982).

Cook, Michael L. *Mystery Fanfare: A Composite Annotated Index to Mystery and Related Fanzines 1963 to 1981.* First edition. Bowling Green State University Popular Press, Bowling Green (1983).

Cook, Michael L. and Miller, Steven T. *Mystery, Detective, and Espionage Fiction: A Checklist of Fiction in U.S. Pulp Magazines, 1915-1974.* First edition. Two volumes. Garland Publishing, Inc., New York (1988).

Hagen, Ordean A. *Who Done It?: A Guide to Detective, Mystery, and Suspense Fiction.* First edition. R.R. Bowker Company. New York (1969). Note: Beware of this book because of its many careless errors.

Hancer, Kevin. *The Paperback Price Guide*. First edition. Overstreet Publications, Inc., Cleveland, TN (1980).

Hubin, Allen J. *The Bibliography of Crime Fiction 1749-1975*. First edition. Publisher's, Inc., Del Mar (1989). All page references in *Double Trouble's* bibliographic material are to this edition.

Hubin, Allen J. *Crime Fiction 1749-1980: A Comprehensive Bibliography*. First edition. Garland Publishing, Inc., New York (1986).

Hubin, Allen J. *1981-1985 Supplement to Crime Fiction 1749-1980*. First edition. Garland Publishing, Inc., New York (1986).

Menendez, Albert J. *The Subject is Murder: A Selective Subject Guide to Mystery Fiction*. First edition. Garland Publishing, Inc., New York (1986).

Pronzini, Bill. *Gun in Cheek: A Study of "Alternative" Crime Fiction*. First edition. Coward, McCann & Geoghegan, New York (1982).

Pronzini, Bill. *Son Of Gun In Cheek*. First edition. The Mysterious Press, New York (1987).

Pronzini, Bill & Muller, Marcia. *1001 Midnights: The Aficionado's Guide to Mystery and Detective Fiction*. First edition. Arbor House, New York (1986).

Reilly, John M., ed. *Twentieth Century Crime and Mystery Writers*. First edition. St. Martin's Press, New York (1980).

Reilly, John M., ed. *Twentieth-Century Crime and Mystery Writers*. Second edition. St. Martin's Press, New York (1985).

Robbins, Leonard A. *The Pulp Magazine Index: First Series*. First edition. Three volumes. Starmont House, Inc., Mercer Island (1989).

Smith, Curtis C. *Twentieth-Century Science-Fiction Writers.* Second edition. St. James Press, Chicago (1986).

Steinbrunner, Chris & Penzler, Otto, eds. *Encyclopedia of Mystery and Detection.* First edition. McGraw-Hill, Inc., New York. (1976).

Vinson, James. *Twentieth-Century Western Writers.* First edition. Gale Research Company, Detroit (1982).

Winn, Dilys, ed. *Murder Ink: The Mystery Reader's Companion.* First edition. Workman Publishing Company, New York (1977).

Winn, Dilys, ed. *Murderess Ink: The Better Half of Mystery.* Reprint edition. Bell Publishing Company, New York (1981).

Dedication

This book is dedicated to my son, Jonathan Bret Jaffery,
on the occasion of his 21st birthday on January 26, 1989,
his graduation from the University of Michigan in May, 1990,
and to applaud his decision to go to medical school.

Acknowledgements

Joe Brockowski, whose index to Ace Paperback Books was invaluable in double-checking the Ace Double Mysteries and made my job much easier, particularily with respect to the tedious task of preparing the Author-Title Index which follows the main body of this work.

Marty Swiatkowski, Dave Bosco and especially one of my favorite pulp collectors (among other of his manias), Walker Martin, for the loan of a number of Ace Mystery Doubles which I was lacking from my collection at the time and without which I couldn't have finished this book.

INTRODUCTION

This won't be a long introduction, nor will it be a maudlin nostalgic piece tearfully raising another glass to a publishing era gone by: an era which memory has gentled; an era admittedly less sophisticated and allegedly less demanding than the one that we presently face each day.

The Ace Double Mystery series was the product of A.A. Wyn, whose publishing experience was earned in the trenches in the heyday of the pulpwood publishers. Wyn, who never met a ten cent pulp he didn't like, had been in the pulp magazine publishing business since the mid 1920s. He picked up the failing *Dragnet* from Harold Hersey in 1930 and promptly changed the title to *Detective-Dragnet* and then to *Ten Detective Aces,* at which point he dropped the price from fifteen cents to a dime, coining the phrase, "A Cent a Story" to emphasize the ten story contents of his brainstorm. His later detective pulps published by Periodical House, Inc., such as *10-Story Detective* and *Secret Agent X,* were similarly priced and stayed that way until the late forties, when rising costs and a changing market necessitated a price increase to fifteen cents.

The Postwar years were tough on the pulps, with sales beginning to decline rapidly. Paperback books, a phenomenon that had emerged in 1939, and television were proving to be too much competition. Street & Smith, always a forerunner in the field, eliminated all of its pulp publications in the summer of 1949, with the exception of *Astounding,* a title which exists today in digest form as *Analog.* That year, A.A. Wyn killed *10-Story Detective* and *Ten Detective Aces.* Several titles of other publishers straggled into the 1950s, including the venerable *Black Mask,* which finally died with the July 1951 issue. A handful of pulps continued to publish into the late fifties for the benefit of an ever-decreasing audience.

Yet the early fifties proved to be the harbinger of a vast alternate market. From the ashes of the once-proud pulps rose the Phoenix of the paperbacks, which was to experience its greatest period of growth as the Korean War raged and died. At first, beginning with the Pocket Book venture in 1939, the emphasis was on reprints, a large amount of which was devoted to detective fiction. More and more original material appeared, however, in the early days of the paperbacks, until, in 1950, Fawcett introduced its Gold Medal line of original novels, a move which probably dealt the final death blow to the pulps. Although some of the Gold Medal original novels were sleazy, other originals featured some excellent material by such authors as Cornell Woolrich, Jim Thompson and John D. MacDonald.

In the midst of the changing nature of the market, A.A. Wyn founded Ace Books, Inc. And that's how we come to this book.

The earliest offerings by the new publishing house were Ace Double Novel Books, which consisted of two novels bound back-to-back, each featuring its own cover. They proclaimed: "Turn this book over for second complete novel." At first, two books were published each month, one being a double mystery and the other a double western. They often combined an original novel with a reprint. Within a year, however, a few non-genre titles crept in, such as D-15, which combined William Lee's (William S. Burroughs) *Junkie* and Maurice Helbrant's *Narcotics Agent,* and D-26, Charles Pettit's *The Impotent General* and *Love in a Junk and Other Exotic Tales* by Harold Acton and Lee Yi-Hsieh. At the same time, the Double Mystery and the Double Western lines were augmented by a Science-Fiction line, a triple-threat combination that lasted until 1963, when Ace phased out the Double Mystery aspect of its publishing list.

The unique thing about the Ace Doubles was not that they were priced at thirty-five cents, no bargain on the surface, as virtually every other publisher at the time required the reader to merely drop a quarter for a copy of their books. Wyn, however, in keeping with the philosophy that had proven to be successful in the pulps, gave the prudent buyer a two-for-one deal. Two books, two covers, seventeen and a half cents each. Who could refuse a deal like that?

The Ace Double line thrived for a number of years under the editorial reins of Donald A. Wollheim, who, as editor-in-chief, supervised all of the books that were published by Ace. Wollheim eventually left Ace to form his own science fiction publishing company, DAW Books, about which more can be learned in my bibliographic retrospective, *Future and Fantastic Worlds* (Starmont House, 1987).

In order to provide two books for not much more than the price of one, corners had to be cut somewhere. Usually it was in the quality of the product itself. Bill Pronzini, in *Gun in Cheek*, his hilarious study of the "alternate," or the worst, in crime fiction, remarked that the Ace Double line had the "most impressive list of alternatives" of any of the publishers doing originals in the early fifties. Geoffrey O'Brien, in *Hardboiled America*, while criticizing Dell's cover art, gave Ace a left-handed compliment (if you want to call it that) when he wrote that Dell's covers "lacked even the trashiness that might have given them some intensity of the kind that abounds in the products of publishers like Ace, Handi-Books, and Graphic. These lower-echelon houses were what people had in mind when they spoke of 'trashy paperbacks.' These were books that virtually guaranteed (by the clear-cut standards of 1954, at any rate) an absence of any redeeming value, literary, social, or otherwise."

I don't agree that Ace Mystery Doubles were, on the whole, trashy, although some may be so classified. Many just weren't very good. O'Brien, on the other hand, sounds like he needs to get laid. Nevertheless, most of the copies of Ace Doubles which I have in my own collection, have yellowing and loose pages, verifying the niggardly quality of the paper and binding methods that characterized the line.

Well, on that note, the canny reader is probably wondering what in the hell I'm doing writing about such a sleazy operation that turned out what some critics would say was among the worst detective fiction of the booming paperback industry of the 1950s. So, I'm a sucker for nostalgia, after all. I love looking at Ace Mystery Doubles, whose covers are so reminiscent of pulp covers, holding them ever so carefully so that the pages don't fall out, and, even if the novels aren't the greatest, I don't care. Nobody has accused me lately of being an intellectual, and, if I ever was, I've forgotten how. My interests, in my middle years, have turned to popular culture, and what better example of the field can there be but Ace Mystery Doubles?

Besides, they're easy to collect since there aren't that many of them (about 130 or so), most of them are inexpensive and not too difficult to find (although I still lack one, Mike Avallone's double offering: D-259, and am still searching), they look good on the shelves, and they're fun to read when one's brain is ready to be turned off.

So, for those of you ready to be snared into entering the wacky world of collecting and, hopefully, reading Ace Mystery Doubles, I can only say that I envy you, I've been there myself, and I've come away a poorer man for the experience.

Sheldon Jaffery
Beachwood, Ohio, 19922

D-SERIES

1952-1961

$.35

D-SERIES   1952-1961 $.35

D-1. ***Too Hot for Hell.*** Vining, Keith. First edition (1952). 134 pp. Cover by Norman Saunders. Hubin, p. 417.

As indicated by the code number, this book is historically significant in that it's the first Ace Original of the Ace Double Novel Books. It's also the only mystery book written by the author, who took the titillating, but campy, concept of *Reefer Madness* and combined marijuana, music, and murder to come up with an otherwise immemorable offering. Depending on condition, a collector will have to pay up to $100.00 for this gem.

• • •

The Grinning Gismo. Taylor, Samuel W. First U.S. paperback edition (1952). 185 pp. Published earlier in U.S. by A.A. Wyn (1951) and in U.K. by Hodder and Stoughton (1952). Cover by Norman Saunders. Hubin, p. 399; also see Pronzini & Muller, *1001 Midnights* pp. 774-775.

This is the first of the unabridged reprints published as one-half of the Ace Double Novel Books. The author wrote only one other suspense novel, also set in San Francisco, *The Man with My Face,* which was published by A.A. Wyn (1948) in the U.S. and by Hodder and Stoughton (1949) in the U.K.

Marcia Muller, who capsulized the plot of the latter novel in *1001 Midnights,* not only noted that it was especially good, but that *The Grinning Gismo* "doesn't come close to measuring up to [*The Man with My Face*]."

My copy of this book isn't worth $100.00. I won't tell you how much I paid for it, but it was too much.

D-3. *The Big Fix.* Colton, Mel (pseud. Hal Braham). First edition (1952). 131 pp. Hubin, p. 91.

The author was an early stalwart of the Ace Double line. This novel was the first of four to be published as half of an Ace Double. A Fifth crime novel was *Big Woman,* published by Magazine Productions (1953). Although Pronzini, in *Gun in Cheek,* doesn't trash Colton, he certainly had him in mind as one of the creators of an alternate brand of postpulp mysteries.

The hero is ballyhooed in a prefatory description of characters as "a private eye with underworld connections, a tough hide, and a dangerously soft heart for the ladies." Well, hell, who wasn't in those days?

*   *   *

Twist the Knife Slowly. Clugston, Kate. First paperback edition (1952). 189 pp. Hubin, p. 86. Published earlier by A. A. Wyn (1947) as *A Murderer in the House.*

"Over-strong sadistic tendencies running amok right within the family circle of an old and quiet homestead near Boston make this latest psychological novel give forth with lots of suspense, bloodshed and that you'd-never-guess-who touch."
—*Tulsa Daily Word*
Another one-shot effort by an Ace author. But not the last.

D-5. *Drawn to Evil.* Whittington, Harry. First edition (1952). 120 pp. Cover by Norman Saunders. Hubin, p. 436.

With this book, Ace at last published a real pro. In fact, Harry Whittington was not only the consummate professional writer, he was so prolific that he came to be known as the king of the paperback originals. Between 1951 and 1963, Whittington had more than 50 crime   novels and some 35 western novels and other genre   fiction published, either under his own name or under one of his many pseudonyms. Although *Drawn to Evil* isn't one of his better-known novels, it was his first to be published by Ace.

* * *

The Scarlet Spade. Goldthwaite, Eaton K. First paperback edition (1952). 184 pp. Cover by Norman Saunders. Hubin, p. 172. Published earlier by Duell, Sloan and Pearce (1951) as *Cut For Partners*.

"Denver Calhoun was a hard man in a tough town. A professional Las Vegas gambler, he's knuckled his way to the top. Yet a sentimental streak in him had kept him gambling on a tramp prospector's endless quest for desert gold. When that old-timer suddenly turned up tortured to death, Denver realized that his grubstake had struck it rich, and a murderer had collected the winnings! Though the stakes were now homicide high, Denver wasn't the type to drop his hand!"

This novel was the only one that the author had published as an Ace Double.

D-7. ***So Dead My Love!*** Whittington, Harry. First edition (1953). 130 pp. Hubin, p.436.

The second Ace Double novel by the fast-paced Whittington, but certainly not the last. The setting is in Florida, a trait common to many of the author's crime novels, and the hero is a private eye from New York.

* * *

I, the Executioner. Ransome, Stephen (pseud. Frederick C. Davis). First U.S. paperback edition (1953). 189 pp. Published earlier in U.S. by Doubleday (1948) and in U.K. by Gollancz (1949) as *False Bounty*. Hubin, p.338

"... I had completed my arrangements for murdering Lydia." "My plan was as lethal as I could make it. I had chosen the same ordinary but effective method used for exterminating lower forms of rodents. I had simply left a deadly trap for Lydia at a spot where she would be most

likely to stick her lovely neck into it. Lydia's death would
not be quick or merciful."

"... I could guarantee her last few hours would be
damned unpleasant ones."

Those lines get this book moving just as if they had
been the opening paragraph or two in a lead novel for
Dime Detective, Black Mask, or *Dime Mystery* during the
heyday of the pulps, where Frederick C. Davis was
published extensively during his career as a pulp writer.
Not only did he produce detective stories, but he wrote
numerous "Operator No. 5" novels, as well as many weird
menace stories for the shudder pulps. In fact, I kicked off
my anthology, *The Weirds,* published by Starmont House
in 1987, with a dynamite yarn from the April-May 1938
issue of *Horror Stories,* Davis' "The Mole Men Want Your
Eyes". Davis often, though not always, used the Stephen
Ransome byline on his non-series novels, of which this is
one.

D-9. *Decoy.* Morgan, Michael (pseud. C. E. Carle and Dean M.
Dorn). First Edition. 165 pp. Hubin, p. 298; Pronzini and Muller,
1001 Murders, pp.580-582; Pronzini, *Gun in Cheek,* pp. 216-223.

This novel had the distinction, for many years, of
being considered by Bill Pronzini the "worst mystery novel
ever written." Evidently, in the course of his research for
Son of Gun in Cheek, the hilarious sequel to *Gun in Cheek,*
Pronzini discovered other "alternative classics" which
challenged the *numero uno* status of *Decoy.* I'd cite some
examples of the alleged prose that adorns nearly every
page of this novel, but Pronzini got all of the good ones.
Unfortunately for the student of the alternative classic, this
was the only Michael Morgan novel published by Ace.
However, the assiduous reader might want to check out the
authors' other two books, *His Kind of Woman,* Pyramid
(1954), and another classic, their very first novel, *Nine More
Lives,* Random House (1947), which was also published as

The Blonde Body, Lion (1949). *Decoy* is a remarkable book in the sense that, after all, it got published.

•   •   •

If I Die Before I Wake. King, Sherwood.   First paperback edition (1953). 154 pp. Hubin, p. 239. Published earlier in U.S. by Simon & Schuster (1938) and in U.K. by World's Work (1938); reprinted by World's Work (1947) as *The Lady from Shanghai.*

"Beautifully written and shocking story of young Laurence Planter, chauffeur for crippled Mr. Bannister and his dynamic, auburn-haired wife. There is a considerable nightmarish quality about this one that will leave [the reader] considerably shaken. The suspense throughout is terrific."
—*New Yorker Magazine*
This is the author's second and last crime novel. His first was *Between Murders* Appleton (1935) as by Sherry King. It was reprinted in the U.K. by Cherry Hill (1941) as *Death Carries a Cane.*

D-11. Mrs. Homicide. Keene, Day. First edition (1953). 152 pp. Hubin, p. 234.

"The whole homicide squad knew their toughest sergeant's wife was cheating on him. They'd seen her themselves, jazzing around the hot spots with a notorious underworld character. But Herman himself didn't know until the moment they picked up 'Mrs. Homicide' drunk and naked in her murdered boy friend's apartment.
The author was another of the prolific pulp writers who regularly appeared in the most prestigious pulp mystery magazines such as *Dime Detective, Detective Tales* and *Black Mask.* In the post pulp period of the fifties, he continued to produce paperback originals for a number of publishers such as Ace, Gold Medal, Graphic, Lion and Avon.

•   •   •

Dead Ahead. Stuart, William L. First paperback edition (1953).
168 pp. Published earlier in U.S. by Rinehart Books, Inc. (1945) as
The Dead Lie Still. Hubin, p. 395.

"This is a mighty tough item about Sam Talbot, artist
and ex-Navy Intelligence, and how he tangles with a bunch
of agents the FBI is trying to round up. Sam proves a
likeable and knowing sleuth, and Mr. Stuart's first novel marks
him as a man to watch. Fast, furious and not for the queasy."
—New Republic

This novel is the first of only two that were written by
this author before he went to Hollywood to pursue a
career as a screen-writer. His second novel was *Night Cry*,
published by Dial (1948), an equally hard-boiled and tough
piece of detective fiction which was put on the screen in
1950 as *Where the Sidewalk Ends*, starring Dana Andrews
and Gene Tierney.

D-17. *Shakedown.* Scott, Roney (pseud. William Campbell Gault).
First edition (1953). 158 pp. Hubin, p. 367.

This novel is the first of seven to feature the series
private eye, Joe Puma. The six subsequent Joe Puma
novels were neither pseudonymous, nor were they
published by Ace.

Gault's other series detective is an ex-jock named
Brock Callahan, a former L.A. Rams player who turned to
crime detection following his football career. An
interesting commingling of the characters occurred in *The
Cana Diversion*, Raven (1982), in which Joe Puma made
a brief appearance—as a corpse—and Callahan got to
search for Puma's murderer.

•   •   •

The Darkness Within. Ericson, Walter (pseud. E.V. Cunningham, in turn the pseudonym of Howard Fast). First paperback edition (1953). 162 pp. Published earlier in hardcover by Little, Brown (1952) as *Fallen Angel* and later in paperback by Fawcett (1965) as *Mirage* as by Howard Fast. Hubin, p.136.

> "A far-above-the-average novel of suspense which is outstanding not only because of the ingenious story but because of the mood and atmosphere that the author creates.... The experience of the reader may be likened to that evoked by Henry James' *Turn of the Screw.*"
> —*Houston Press*

That's some healthy praise for the prolific Howard Fast's first crime novel, albeit two pseudonyms removed from his own name, which was still slightly tarnished after Fast was imprisoned in 1947 for contempt of Congress.

In 1965, not only was the novel reprinted as *Mirage,* but Gregory Peck and Walter Matthau co-starred in a film of the same name which had been made from the novel.

D-19. *Never Kill a Cop.* Colton, Mel (pseud. Hal Braham). First edition (1953). 147 pp. Hubin, p.91.

> "Even under ordinary circumstances, Danny Harrington would have rated as a tough cop, afraid of nothing and a demon with his fists. Add the fact that Danny's brother was the boss of the city's ruthless political machine which rode roughshod over the department and could and did force Danny's premature advancement, and you have the makings of trouble.
>
> Although Danny objected to the way things were 'greased' for him, this couldn't prevent the steadily growing resentment of his fellow officers. So, when Danny's brother was tossed off his throne by an underworld upheaval at the same time that Danny

accidently killed a ward-heeler in a night club brawl, the cops went all out to get them both—with no holds barred."

This novel was the first of two Colton originals published by Ace in 1953.

* * *

Fear No More. Edgley, Leslie. First U.S. paperback edition (1953). 173 pp. Published earlier in U.S. by Simon & Schuster (1946) and in U.K. by Barker (1948). Hubin, p. 132.

> "For a moment her throat was so constricted she felt weak with nausea. The grey, sallow face seemed to twitch impatiently; the pudgy jaws stopped chewing....It was like a terrifying dream in the hazy suspension between sleeping and waking...."

This novel, about which Anthony Boucher said, "For macabre tension, it's one of the best yet...," was Edgley's second to be published by Ace. His first, an interesting little gem called *The Judas Goat,* is the flip side of Ace Double D-13, published together with *Cry Plague!* by Theodore S. Drachman, M.D. earlier in 1953. Oddly, D-13 has always been bibliographically included in the Ace Science Fiction Double series and is one of the scarcer and more expensive collectibles. I say "oddly" because *The Judas Goat* is definitely a mystery yarn, and *Cry Plague!* is only marginally science fiction. In fact, Hubin lists it in his crime fiction bibliography. Honest. You could check it out.

D-21. ***Nightshade.*** Makris, John N. First edition (1953). 131 pp. Cover by Norman Saunders. Hubin, p. 277.

> Nightshade: a strong-scented, narcotic, beautiful plant, with poisonous leaves.

> "She was as cunning as she was beautiful. She knew all the tricks in the book; how to make a man aid her in

her money-hungry treacheries, how to leave him helpless when she was through. But when her ambitions led to cold-blooded murder, the last remnants of Ken Martin's love turned to hate, and he set out on a desperate search for freedom through vengeance."

The author's only crime novel.

* * *

High Stakes. Dent, Lester. First U.S. paperback edition (1953). 187 pp. Published earlier in U.S. by Doubleday (1946) and in U.K. by Cassell (1948) as *Dead at the Take-off.* Hubin, p. 117; Pronzini & Muller, *1001 Midnights,* pp. 199-200.

"There isn't much mystery in this thriller; you always know who killed whom. But Chance Molloy's fight against ruthless Senator Lord for the airline Molloy had built up in South America is ruggedly put forward, the action is practically all aboard a plane, and the entire treatment is refreshingly clever."

—*Boston Daily Globe*

According to Herbert Ruhm, in his introduction to *The Hard-Boiled Detective,* Dent felt that the departure of Cap Shaw from the editorial helm of *Black Mask Magazine* kept him from becoming a fine writer. Dent had had published over 200 Doc Savage novels under his pseudonym, Kenneth Robeson, and evidently looked upon them and other pulp work as "reams of saleable crap." There were only two stories that he really cared about, "Sail" and "Angelfish," both of which constituted his sole contributions to *Black Mask.* Yet the pair are considered classics of the hard-boiled school and exemplify the *Black Mask* tradition.

This novel, Dent's first to appear under his own name, is considered by some to be his best. It was one of two published in 1946 which featured Chance Molloy. The other was *Lady to Kill,* also published by Doubleday (1946) in the U.S. and by Cassell (1949) in the U.K.

D-23. *Bring Back Her Body.* Brock, Stuart (pseud. Louis Trimble).
First edition (1953). 142 pp. Hubin, p. 50.

    "'I want Paula or her body—I don't care which.' This
was the command of her wealthy, ruthless father. But Abel
Cain, who undertook the search, found that he had been
presented with only one side of the ugly truth. There were
others looking for the hidden heiress too, and among them
were the forces of jealousy, greed, and murderous
vengeance."
    "When an island orgy held by Paula's friends backfired
and the two-faced revelers uncovered a surprise coffin,
Cain found the key to his puzzle, one that pointed to
something terribly simple and utterly evil."
    This was the first novel by Louis Trimble published by
Ace. It was the only one under the Stuart Brock alias.
Trimble's novelistic output totaled more than sixty,
although his best work was in the western genre.
Nevertheless, his books, whether western, science fiction
or mystery, are entertaining. He is well represented in the
Ace line, particularly in the late fifties and early sixties.
Phoenix had been his primary publisher in the forties, with
an occasional book published by Lion Books.

                          *   *   *

Passing Strange. Sale, Richard. First paperback edition (1953).
176 pp. Published earlier by Simon & Schuster (1942). Hubin, p. 361.

    Will Cuppy, mystery reviewer for the New York
Herald-Tribune, said of this novel:
    "To the best of our knowledge and belief, it is the first
thriller in which a Hollywood gynecologist is shot three
times and killed while another medico is performing an
operation upon a movie star in the same room. Some
situation, what?"
    The plot described by Cuppy isn't too surprising when
one realizes that Sale began writing mystery fiction in the
early thirties for such pulps as *Super Detective, 10
Detective Aces* and *Detective Fiction Weekly.* This novel
features police detective Daniel Webster, who was Sale's

series character in his longer work. In the shorter stories in the pulps, series characters were Joe "Daffy" Dill, Bill Hanly, Candid Jones and Lieutenant Alec Mason.

Sale wrote many screen plays and television plays and directed a number of "B" movies, such as *Campus Honeymoon* (1948) and *Gentlemen Marry Brunettes* (1955).

D-27. *Double Take*. Colton, Mel (pseud. Hal Braham). First edition (1953). 136 pp. Hubin, p. 91.

"A knife stuck in a pal's back is not easy to forget, and neither is a girl who's willing to play with fire yet is afraid of the dark. That's why Danny Sherman ignored the advice to stay in his own backyard with the plug-uglies, the failures and the small-time crooks. Even though it was a big-shot hood like Mike Mantouri who had warned him.

"Though the case took Danny out of the two-bit dives into the lush surroundings of such night spots as Mike's Golden Spade, he learned fast that the kind of million-dollar lovelies who hung out there were deadlier than any character he had ever crossed along Skid Row."

Double Take was the second Colton novel published by Ace in 1953.

* * *

The Fingered Man. Fischer, Bruno. First U.S. paperback edition (1953). 182 pp. Cover by Norman Saunders. Hubin, p. 146. Published earlier in U.S. by Doubleday (1944) as *Quoth the Raven* and in U.K. by Quality Press (1947) as *Croaked the Raven*.

Fischer has about twenty-five crime novels to his credit. Under his own name and as Russell Gray, however, he turned out hundreds of short stories for the pulps. A regular contributor to virtually every detective pulp, it was in that market that he began signing his own name to his work.

During the thirties, much of Fischer's output was destined for the "shudder" pulps, a term coined by the late

pulp historian, Bob Jones. There, under the pseudonym of
Russell Gray, appeared numerous stories in magazines such
as *Terror Tales, Horror Stories,* and *Dime Mystery.* Probably
the best things about the earlier stories were the titles. Don't
you wish you could have read such epics as "The Curse
of the Swollen Ones," "The Man Who Loved a Zombie,"
"Slaves for the Wine Goddess," and "Girls for the Pain
Dance"? The last title, incidentally, was typical of the offerings which were gathered under the sub-genre which
can be best described as "sex and sadism" stories. Russell
Gray and Donald Graham were among the most prolific of
the writers who catered to the readers' taste in that area.

   The Fingered Man was published by Ace in a "Specially
Edited Edition," which, translated, means that the guts were
torn out by abridgement. The *Saturday Review of Literature* gave high marks to the novel, stating: "Plentiful action,
good characters, and sinuous plot...."

D-29. *The Fast Buck.* Laurence, Ross. First edition (1953). 132
pp. Hubin, p. 247.

   "Ten will get you twenty. Ten grand will get you twenty
grand...overnight.'
   "This was the bait on the hook—and it worked. Earn-
ing peanuts as a two-bit slugger, Joe Chicago had quit
dreaming about grabbing on to the big money. Then the
break came: a chance to pick up a small fortune for practically nothing—or so Joe thought.
   "But a well-planned swindle that involved a collection
of priceless sapphires didn't have room for small fry. And
Joe found himself marked off as a dead man, with nothing left but his own raw guts to help him fight his way back
to the world of the living."
   The Fast Buck is a typical tough-guy novel of the early
fifties, the kind that might have been made into a "B"
movie. This was the author's only crime novel.

• • •

Dead Man Friday. Hutton, J.F. First U.S. paperback edition (1953). 186 pp. Hubin, p. 219. Published earlier in U.S. by Simon & Schuster (1948) as *Too Good to be True* and in U.K. by Foulsham (1949) as *The Dolphin Mystery.*

"Refreshingly different kind of sleuth, working against a colorful background and some mighty odd people...with diverting byways that don't hurt the plot."
—*Saturday Review of Literature*
This was the author's first book and her only crime novel .

D-33. *Murder by the Pack.* Hodges, Carl G. First edition (1953). 147 pp. Cover by Norman Saunders. Hubin, p. 207.

Bill Pronzini, in *Gun in Cheek,* memorialized an earlier novel by Hodges, *Naked Villainy,* his first, published by Farrell Publishing Company in 1951, as the last of a three book venture into original crime fiction under its "Suspense Novel" imprint. Hodges' third and last in the field was *Crime on My Hands,* published by Phantom Books (1953). Phantom fared somewhat better than Farrell, publishing fourteen digest-sized crime novels in the early fifties, of which four were authored by Day Keene.

As an aside, Farrell also published a digest magazine which lasted but four issues from Spring 1951 through Winter 1952 and was allegedly inspired by the CBS radio and television series, Suspense. The short-lived venture included stories by such diverse writers as Ray Bradbury, Fritz Leiber, A.E. van Vogt, Brett Halliday and John Dickson Carr.

Pronzini quoted some great alternate passages from Hodges' earlier book. However, *Murder by the Pack* has some goodies of its own. Not too shabby are the words that issued from the lips of the police lieutenant who, for the first time, met the hero, Bob Ruff, at the scene of a murder. Upon being given a calling card by the protagonist (don't all private dicks carry calling cards, for God's sake? Mike Hammer, eat your heart out.):

"...O'Malley saw the two words in the corner and he read them off like he was telling a dirty story. 'Private investigations. So? You're one of those masterminds. You're a P.I. A private eye. One of those guys that's always showing up the cops as a bunch of nitwits. Rough and tough. Rockem-sockem. Lady Killer. Sure, you're rough and tough. Your name's even Ruff."

Snappy, scathing, sarcastic stuff, n'est ce pas?

*   *   *

About Face. Kane, Frank. Reprint (1953) 172 pp. Published earlier by Curl (1947) and as *Death About Face* by Quinn Publishing Co. (Handi Book series) (1948); published later by Dell (1958) as *The Fatal Foursome.* Hubin, p. 230. See also Pronzini & Muller, *1001 Midnights,* p. 422.

This novel was Kane's first, as well as being the first Johnny Liddell novel. Liddell, Kane's popular, fast-talking, wise-cracking, hard-boiled private eye with a taste for redheads, lasted through twenty-nine novels, most of which were paperback originals and sold more than five million copies over the life of the series. One of the trademarks of the series were the puns in the titles, such as *Slay Ride, Trigger Mortis, A Short Bier,* and *Time to Prey.*

Kane first featured Liddell in the pulps in *Crack Detective* and later graduated to *Manhunt, The Saint,* and *Mike Shayne Mystery Magazine* when the pulps died out in favor of digest sized detective magazines. During the forties, he was also writing radio scripts for *The Shadow, The Fat Man* and *Gangbusters.* Later he scripted for the *Mike Hammer* TV series and maintained the same lean, hard-boiled style.

About Face was the only Frank Kane novel published by Ace.

D-37. *The Drowning Wire.* Claire, Marvin. First edition (1953). 156 pp. Hubin, p. 83.

"I'm Joe. I'm Joe Haugen. I'm not a big guy in these parts. Not big in the way most people think. I guess I stand around six foot two or three. I'm not sure which and it don't make any difference. I'm a trapper up here. I trap in the winter and I fish in the summer. I like my life and I wouldn't give it up for anything in the world. Not even for ten thousand dollars and a whore."

I'm Sheldon. I'm Sheldon Jaffery. I like books. I don't like all books. I especially don't like books that start out like this one. I don't care whether Joe Haugen is six foot two or three. I don't care when he traps and fishes. I think he's stupid. Ten thousand dollars and a whore sounds like a pretty good price to me.

This crime novel was written by Marvin. It was written by Marvin Claire. This was the only crime novel written by Marvin Claire. I would have given Marvin ten thousand dollars and a whore not to write another crime novel. He did it for free. I like that very much.

•   •   •

Departure Delayed. Oursler, Will. First paperback edition thus (1953). 164 pp. Hubin, p. 316. Published earlier by Simon & Schuster (1947) and as *Bullets for a Blonde* in digest size by Bestseller (1949).

"Suffering with what appears to be amnesia, Roy Marshall suddenly recovers to find that he got into a peck of trouble while walking around as Johnny Wilson. He had married a society girl and walked out on her, then mixed with synthetic blonde (sic), and the cops think he murdered a man. Stick with it and you'll enjoy Mr. Oursler's skill in developing new angles. Tease routines involve Roy's war adventures, a villain who's after the lad, jail, a friendly G-2 man called Spike Yamada and mysterious old Mr. Lazarus."
—*New York Herald-Tribune*

Departure Delayed is one of four crime novels written under the author's real name. Pseudonyms were Nick Marino and, jointly with Margaret Scott, Gale Gallagher.

D-40. Scylla. Bishop, Malden Grange. First edition (1954). 127 pp. Hubin, p. 34.

"She was just Scylla Zubitch, a girl with a beautiful body and nothing else of value, and this man patting her leg was just another man who wanted the only thing she had to offer anyone."

This book is the author's only crime novel. It's sexy, with a sexy cover, and more like a Lion Book than an Ace. After all, a girl named Scylla Zubitch has to have something going for her.

* * *

Waltz into Darkness. Irish, William (pseud. Cornell Woolrich). First U.S. paperback edition (1954). (Abridged). 191 pp. Published earlier in U.S. by Lippincott (1947) and in U.K. by Hutchinson (1948). Hubin, p. 221.

During the thirties, Cornell Woolrich wrote only for pulp magazines such as *Black Mask* and *Detective Fiction Weekly*. His first novel, *The Bride Wore Black*, kicked off his "Black" series of novels and was followed by *The Black Curtain, Black Alibi, The Black Angel, The Black Path of Fear*, and *Rendezvous in Black*.

Writing also as George Hopley and William Irish, Woolrich produced magnificent novels and short stories, many of which were adapted into film, radio and television dramatic presentations.

Waltz into Darkness, set in latter-day New Orleans, is classified by Peter Lovesey in his article for *Murder Ink* as an historical mystery. The novel was the basis for the 1969 United Artists film, *The Mississippi Mermaid*, with Jean-Paul Belmondo and the luscious Catherine Deneuve. The film was directed by Truffaut.

D-41. *Death House Doll.* Keene, Day. First edition (1954). 140 pp. Hubin, p. 234.

"Mona Ambler sat in the death house with a secret that not even a decent guy like Mike Duval could extract. Just home from Korea, Mike had to go about saving the gal the hard way. Maybe she really had shot and killed a jewelry salesman, maybe she had been the no-good thieving B-girl the papers had reported. but just the same she had also been the beloved wife of Mike's only brother.

"The odds were a hundred-to-one that Mona would go to the chair without talking. But Mike Duval was willing to gamble against these odds. The thing he didn't realize was that the boss of the city rackets was betting against him with every gunman, chiseler, and grafter on his side. Because Mona knew something that could blast the city wide open!"

Keene's fast-paced style made him one of the more popular writers of paperback originals. Not noted for innovative plotting, he was able to take familiar themes and add new and unexpected elements, thereby keeping the reader interested to the end.

• • •

Mourning After. Dewey, Thomas B. First U.S. paperback edition (1954). 180 pp. Published earlier in the U.S. by Mill (1950) and in the U.K. by Dakers (1953). Hubin, p. 119.

"Skillfully compounds intrigue, beautiful women, the ruthless political boss and Singer Batts into a complex mystery that taxes the skill of the best reader-detective."
—*Gadsden Times*

Dewey, during his prolific writing career, which included 36 crime novels, featured three major series characters: Singer Batts, Mac, and Pete Schofield. Singer Batts was his first hero, being featured in four of the author's first five books, thereafter falling to the wayside in favor of the more popular Mac, a Sam Spade/Philip Marlowe/Lew Archer kind of private eye. Interspersed with his later Mac novels, however, were the lighter-toned Pete Schofield novels.

As was the case with other of the better crime novelists of the fifties, this was the only Dewey appearance in an Ace double.

D-45. *Death Hitches a Ride.* Weiss, Martin L. First edition (1954). 124 pp. Hubin, p. 429.

"Alvin Hopkins rode with death in more ways than one. As a narcotics agent in New Orleans, he'd just barely escaped being murdered. His superiors assigned him to sunny California, so Alvin kissed his dancer girl friend good-by, though he soon found that he hadn't seen the last of that lovely.

"But his troubles began in dead earnest when Alvin gave a lift to a couple of headstrong young chaps. They turned out to have a private mission of their own and it had nothing to do with getting to California safely—or even alive!"

The author had but two crime novels to his credit, both published by Ace as originals. The second was *Hate Alley,* published in 1957.

• • •

Tracked Down. Edgley, Leslie. First U.S. paperback edition (1954). 194 pp. Published earlier by Doubleday (1947) and Barker (1949) as *The Angry Heart.* Hubin, p. 132.

"M.'s principal source of graft came from shaking down prostitutes; an expert in framing young girls...

"Curt Prentice returned from abroad to find his beautiful young wife had been framed by a crooked cop and was now listed as a suicide. Trying to defend her, her brother had been 'shot while resisting arrest.'

"M. always prided self on high number of arrests and harsh treatment of prisoners...

"Curt nearly went crazy with grief and horror, with the burning desire for vengeance. He got hold of a pistol. But the cop had already been tossed off the force, had moved to another state.

"M.'s association with vice syndicate definitely proved...

"Curt took that pistol, loaded it, started out. He tracked M. down across two thousand miles and a dozen states, finally cornered him in a Hollywood art gallery!

"M.'s record marked by brutality, graft; arrested over a thousand women...

"And then—while Curt's finger trembled on the trigger—murder struck from elsewhere and Curt found himself an involuntary guest in M.'s own home and the chosen defender of M.'s own innocent daughter!

"This is a tense, fast-moving story of tragedy in a California art circle, skilfully written. Vastly exciting."

—*Providence Journal*

D-47. *Kiss and Kill.* Barry, Joe (pseud. Joe Barry Lake). First edition (1954). 147 pp. Hubin, p. 25.

"What had happened to be only a routine assignment had led unexpectedly to the kiss-and-kill death of Donn O'Meara's partner. And when Donn took up the trail of the dame with the deadly embrace, he hadn't suspected that it would land him straight in the center of a war between crime syndicates.

"By that time it was too late to back out. Face to face with Mr. Big himself, Donn found that he was on a one-way street to the morgue. Then it was that he met that lethal girl again!"

Kiss and Kill does not feature the author's primary series character, Rush Henry, who appeared in four novels published by Mystery House during the mid-forties: *The Pay-Off* (1943), *The Third Degree* (1943), *The Fall Guy* (1945), and *The Triple Cross* (1946). The author had no other novels but this one published by Ace Books.

*   *   *

On the Hook. Powell, Richard. First U.S. paperback edition
(1954). 172 pp. Published earlier as *Shark River* in U.S. by Simon
& Schuster (1950) and in U.K. by Hodder & Stoughton (1951).
Hubin, p. 331.

> Richard Powell wrote several novels featuring Arab and
> Andy Blake as series characters. This book, the only Powell
> crime novel published by Ace Books, is not one of those.
> Need I say more? Can I say more?

D-49. *Tongking!* Cushman, Dan. First edition (1954). 132 pp.
Hubin, p.106.

> The author wrote a number of "jungle thrillers" as Gold
> Medal Originals during the fifties. He penned such exotic
> works as *Jewel of the Java Sea*(1951), *Savage Interlude*
> (1952), *Jungle She* (1953), *Port Orient* (1955), and *The
> Forbidden Land* (1958).
> *Tongking!* is a story of gun smuggling and illicit love
> on Red China's pirate coast.
> But enough about this book. Now I get to plug one of
> my other loves of popular fiction, the pulps. Cushman was
> a steady contributor to one of my favorite pulps, *Northwest
> Romances*. In case you think I've freaked out, fear not.
> Subtitled "Stories of the Wilderness Frontier," this dandy
> pulp wasn't a "love" magazine. With settings primarily in
> Alaska and Canada, the pulp regularly published adventure
> stories and poetry by the likes of Jack London and Robert
> Service. Frederick L. Nebel, who merely wrote more than
> sixty stories for *Black Mask*, was also an occasional
> contributor.
> Why, the cynical reader may ask, do I like Dan
> Cushman's work so much, particularly in such an offbeat
> pulp as *Northwest Romances?* I thought you'd never ask.
> How could I pass up stories with titles such as "Buckskin

Loot for Lobo-Men," "Voyageurs of the Midnight Sun," "Death to the Red-Coat Tyrant!," and "Malemute Breed"? Trust me on this. Try Cushman if you can find him in the pulps. You'll like him. You'll probably even like *Tongking!* if you read it.

* * *

Golden Temptress. Grayson, Charles. First U.S. Paperback edition (1954). (Abridged edition). 186 pp. Published earlier by Doubleday (1948) as *The Broken Gate.*

The reader won't find a reference to this novel in Hubin, as it isn't a crime novel. What the hell is it doing in this bibliography, for God's sake? It happened to be attached to the Cushman book, and I thought I'd throw it in for W. Somerset Maugham lovers, if its reviews can be trusted.

"...so rich-hued and moving a tale of exotic Indo-China that I warmly recommend it to escapees in the eerie hours....The adventures there are Maughamish—with sun on silk, moon on palm, gold on green baize, and love and hate playing across town in taxi and ricksha...This is a whale of a good yarn."
—Nashville Tennessean

D-51. *Switcheroo.* McDowell, Emmett. First edition (1954). 142 pp. A magazine version appeared in 1953 as "The Tattooed Nude" in *Triple Detective Magazine.* Hubin, p.269.

The author had four crime novels and a collection of three crime novelets published by Ace Books from 1954 to 1960, of which *Switcheroo* was the first. All of the books but this one featured Jonathan Knox. The lead character in this novel is Jaimie MacRae, described as "a private eye with bunions on the feet and a blonde on the brain." That's better, I suppose, than the other way around.

* * *

Over the Edge. Treat, Lawrence. First paperback edition (1954).
(Specially edited edition). 176 pp. Published earlier in U.S. by Wil-
liam Morrow & Co. (1948) and later in U.K. by Boardman (1958).
Hubin, p. 407.

This novel combines the talents of two of Lawrence
Treat's series characters, Jub Freeman, a scientific detective
operating out of the police lab, and Homicide Lieutenant
Bill Decker. The author was a pioneer in the sub-genre of
police procedural fiction and paved the way for the popular
87th Precinct novels by Ed McBain (Evan Hunter) and
Elizabeth Linington, who also wrote procedural novels as
Dell Shannon and Lesley Egan.

"Empaneled as foreman of a jury to try a man for
pushing his wife off a cliff, Alec Rambeau, hard-drinking,
but smart public relations counselor, quickly realizes that
he himself had been the murdered woman's lover. Her mild
professor husband is convicted. But the thing weighs
heavily with Alec. He reopens the case...the story packs
continuing suspense to a spine-chilling climax.

"Whether writing of cops or homicide, or cabbies, or
businessmen or gals, Treat makes his people convincing
and his dialogues sound like human beings talking...."
—*San Diego Union*

D-55. *The Tobacco Auction Murders.* Turner, Robert. First edition (1954). 131 pp. Hubin, p. 410.

"Suddenly uneasy, Jake Krane came South in search of
his strangely silent wife. Vickie's last letter had hinted at a
mysterious desperation. But Jake arrived at Wilsboro, N.C.
just a bit too late—for not even his horror and anger could
bring Vickie from her swampy grave."
This is one of three crime novels written by the author,
of which two were published by Ace as originals. The other

Ace offering was *The Girl in the Cop's Pocket* (1956). The third, *The Night Is For Screaming,* was brought out by Pyramid (1960). Turner's only other crime-related book was a collection of short stories, titled *Shroud 9,* published by Powell (1970).

*   *   *

Kill-Box. Stark, Michael (pseud. Lawrence Lariar). First U.S. paperback edition (1954). 187 pp. Published earlier in U.S. by Crown (1946) and in U.K. by Boardman (1948) as *Run for Your Life!*. Hubin, p. 388.

This crime novel was the only one published by Lawrence Lariar under this pseudonym. Eight others were published under his own name, of which four featured the character, Homer Bull.

D-59. *Spiderweb.* Bloch, Robert. First edition (1954). 157 pp. Hubin, pp. 37-38.

Nothing can be added to the legend of a man, now 75 years young, who claims "I have the heart of a small boy; I keep it in a jar on my desk." Bob Bloch's wit and humor is as fresh today as it has been for many of the more than fifty years that he has been making professional sales (the first at the age of seventeen to the legendary *Weird Tales.*)

Although a great deal of Bloch's output has been in the weird, macabre and horror genres, he has contributed several masterworks to the area of the criminous, particularly in his treatment of the psychological, even, perhaps, psychopathic, thriller. His first novel was *The Scarf,* published by Dial Press in 1948 as *The Scarf of Passion.* I related an interesting anecdote in my Arkham House bibliographies, *The Arkham House Companion* (Starmont House, 1989) and *Horrors and Unpleasantries* (Popular Press, 1982), as to how Bloch's career changed due to August Derleth's publication of his first collection of short stories, *The Opener of the Way*. Bloch had written me:

"When *The Opener of the Way* was about to go to press I received a somewhat frantic letter from Derleth—incredible as it might seem today, he was worried then that the book might not be quite long enough to justify its $3.00 price-tag! And could I please come up with an extra story for immediate inclusion? After surveying the balance of my published material I wasn't able to find an additional yarn which satisfied me, so there was no alternative; I sat down and wrote the final story, "One Way to Mars." It appeared in *Weird Tales* just prior to the appearance of the collection, I believe, and this hastily-written story, dashed out at Derleth's urgent insistence, became the very first major departure from my usual style and my first real venture into the psychological horror area. Unwittingly, Derleth had turned me around and launched me on a new orbit. Less than a year later, I began work on my first novel, *The Scarf,* and he, in no small measure, is to blame for everything that followed."

After the publication of *The Scarf,* there was a hiatus of seven years before another novel appeared. *Spiderweb,* a story about a phony California cult, was one of three Bloch crime novels to be published in 1954, two of which were published by Ace as originals. The third, *The Kidnapper,* was a Lion Book (1954).

*   *   *

The Corpse in My Bed.   Alexander, David.   First U.S. paperback edition (1954). (Abridged edition). 161 pp. Published earlier in U.S. by Random House (1951) and in U.K. by Hammond (1953) as *Most Men Don't Kill*. Hubin, p. 5.

"A bare body with a hole in its heart greets amateur detective Terry Rooke when he returns to his hotel room. The room was supposed to be a private peephole from which he could gather evidence about the gal—evidence her husband is paying for. But the gal meandered in, lost her wardrobe and her wits, and ended up murdered."
—*Omaha World-Herald*

"It's a rough, tough story, with fast dialogue."
—*Louisville Courier-Journal*
This novel combines two of the author's series characters, amateur private eye Terry Rooke and Tommy Twotoes, an oddball penguin fancier, with a cameo appearance by a third, Lieutenant Romano of the Homicide Squad.

D-63. *You'll Die Next!* Whittington, Harry. First edition (1954). 117 pp. Published later in U.K. by Red Seal (1959). Hubin, p. 436.

"Henry Wilson believed in love. He had to, because why else would Lila have married him? She could have had everything: swanky clothes, high-priced cars—the works. Instead she chose Henry, his rundown cottage, his old jalopy.

"Then one morning the sky fell on Henry's head and he found himself confronting a side of Lila he could never accept. And in the midst of his horror, he awoke to a nightmare from which there seemed no escape, a nightmare that made Henry the frenzied target of an entire city's murderous wrath."

This is a fast-paced thriller by the prolific writer of early paperback originals. Whittington also wrote numerous novels as Ashley Carter, Whit Harrison, Hallam Whitney, Tabor Evans and Robert Hart Davis, among other pseudonyms.

• • •

Drag the Dark. Davis, Frederick C. First U.S. paperback edition (1954). 201 pp. Published earlier in U.S. by Doubleday (1953) and in U.K. by Gollancz (1954) as by Stephen Ransome. Hubin, p. 111.

Davis was one of the most prolific of pulp writers, rivalling other masters of the genre such as Max Brand, Arthur J. Burks, Norman Daniels, and Walter B. Gibson in sheer quantity of output. He knocked out about a thousand stories over a career that spanned more than twenty-five years. Even at the usual wage scale of a penny a word,

Davis was able to make a comfortable living from his writing during the dark days of the depression years. He started writing novels for Doubleday in 1938 and authored more than thirty-five under his own name and his primary pseudonym, Stephen Ransome.

Drag the Dark featured the team of Schyler Cole and Luke Speare, a semi-hard-boiled detective team. Other novels in the Cole and Speare series were *The Deadly Miss Ashley* (1950), *Lilies in Her Garden Grew* (1951), *Tread Lightly. Angel* (1952), *Another Morgue Heard From* (1954), and *Night Drop* (1955).

D-71. *Drop Dead!.* Ashe, Gordon (pseud. John Creasey). First U.S. edition (1954). 161 pp. Published earlier in U.K. by Long (1953) as *The Long Search*. Hubin, p. 15.

Talk about prolificacy! John Creasey wrote about 560 novels under more than twenty names. As Gordon Ashe alone, he wrote more than fifty, all of which, save two, featured Patrick Dawlish and "The Crime Haters." Other series characters under his own name as well as his many pseudonyms include such well-known detectives as The Toff, The Baron, Roger West and, of course, as J.J. Marric, Creasey created the character of Gideon of Scotland Yard, my personal favorite for which he has achieved critical acclaim as the unrivaled master of the British procedural novel.

This Ace double is the first to combine two reprint novels, instead of featuring an original with a reprint. In fact, there is no indication on the book that *Drop Dead!* had ever been published before, much less under its British title of *The Long Search*. The novel is set in America and, more specifically, in the Grand Canyon. Perhaps it was the American flavor that led this novel to be the first Patrick Dawlish adventure to be published in the United States.

•   •   •

The Case of the Hated Senator. Scherf, Margaret. First paperback edition (1954). 156 pp. Published earlier by Doubleday (1953) as *Dead: Senate Office Building*. Hubin, p. 366.

> "If you have in mind some Congressional gentleman who, you think, should be done in in a particularly nasty manner this tale is your meat...."
> —*Brattleboro Daily Reformer*

Although the author had several series characters, the most popular being the Reverend Martin Buell of the Episcopalian Christ Church in Farrington, Montana, *The Case of the Hated Senator* was one of her non-series mysteries and the only one to be reprinted as half of an Ace Double. Other non-series mysteries were *The Corpse Grows a Beard* (Putnam, 1940), *The Case of the Kippered Corpse* (Putnam, 1941) and *Don't Wake Me Up While I'm Driving* (Doubleday, 1977).

D-77. ***Stranger at Home.*** Sanders, George. First U.S. paperback edition (1954). 174 pp. Published earlier in U.S. by Simon & Schuster (1946) and in U.K. by Pilot Press (1947). Hubin, p. 362.

George Sanders, the noted film star who played many a tough character, including The Saint, as well as character parts as suave British gentlemen, had two crime novels credited to him, of which *Stranger at Home* was the second. Neither novel was written by Sanders.

The first, *Crime on My Hands,* published by Simon & Schuster in 1944, was ghost-written by Craig Rice and Cleve Cartmill. The Ace publication was dedicated: "To Leigh Brackett, Whom I Have Never Met." I presume that Sanders wrote the dedication himself. Guess who wrote the book?

Brackett combined those elements that she knew well: Los Angeles, private eyes and the movies, into a novel about which the St. Louis Post-Dispatch enthused: "The characters are hardboiled, the language colorful and the solution elusive."

I wonder why Sanders never had any more novels written for him. Maybe it was a case of ghost-writer's block.

* * *

Catch the Brass Ring. Marlowe, Stephen (pseud. Milton Lesser). First edition (1954). 146 pp. Hubin, p. 281.

The author, as Milton Lesser, wrote primarily in the science fiction field. This interest later carried over into his mystery writing, which was published, for the most part, under the Stephen Marlowe pseudonym. In some of his later works, such as *Translation* (1977) and *The Valkyrie Encounter* (1978), science fiction elements appear.

Catch the Brass Ring was the first Marlowe mystery, and, while his later novels are generally better, remains an excellent early work.

The cover of the book proclaims that it is "Complete and Unabridged." The proclamation is a mystery in its own right, since the novel is an Ace original, never having been published before.

D-81. *Too Many Sinners.* Stark, Sheldon. First edition (1954). 165 pp. Hubin, p. 388.

"It was a perfect blackmail gimmick for a fear-ridden industry. You couldn't fight it—either you paid up or you were kicked off the air. It was a holier-than-thou scandal sheet called *The Moralist,* and TV director Don Brandon knew that to be mentioned in its pages was the kiss of death.

"But Don was never able to make the demanded payoff. Someone had beaten him to the lethal punch, and Don arrived in time to make himself the object of a manhunt that turned a shocked city against him. He was boxed in and the lid was about to be lowered."

This crime novel was the author's one and only. Perhaps he got mentioned by those other TV "moralists," Jim Bakker and Jimmy Swaggart.

• • •

Liability Limited. Saxon, John A. First U.S. paperback edition (1954). 155 pp. Published earlier in U.S. by Mill (1947) and in U.K. by Foulsham (1947), the latter under the title of *This Was No Accident*. Hubin, p. 365.

Saxon, who died in 1947, had two books published that year, both of which featured Sam Welpton, an insurance claims adjustor, as their protagonist. The other title was *Half-Past Mortem,* Mill (1947), which, interestingly enough, was not written by Saxon. It was ghost-written by Robert Leslie Bellem, the creator of the famed Dan Turner, Hollywood Detective. Bellem, one of the most prolific pulp writers of the thirties and forties under a variety of pseudonyms, often produced more than a million words a year with numerous stories appearing in the "spicies," i.e. *Spicy Detective, Spicy Mystery, Spicy Western* and *Spicy Adventures,* as well as other pulps such as *Popular Detective* and *Private Detective*. If anyone could claim the title of "King of the Spicies," it was Bellem.

Bellem also received plenty of ink from Bill Pronzini in *Gun in Cheek* and *Son of Gun in Cheek* for such sparkling anatomical references as "She swayed toward me, a sob swelling her perky pretty-pretties" and "The swim suit's brassiere top had cupped the niftiest set of plumply domed whatchacallems this side of a castaway's dream."

S. J. Perelman was a fan of Robert Leslie Bellem and Dan Turner, his "private skulk," capturing the essence of the Bellem charm in an essay titled "Somewhere a Roscoe..." With Bellem, guns were rods, heaters, or roscoes. They didn't fire, they barked, sneezed or stuttered. They didn't go "Bang," they went "Chow-Chow", "Ka-Chow", "Chowp", and "Blooey," sometimes several strange sounds at once, such as "a roscoe sneezed: Ka-Chow! Chowpf!" Check out *Gun in Cheek*. I highly recommend it. I don't have the space to do justice to the wonderful world of Robert Leslie Bellem, and I certainly couldn't top Bill Pronzini in his selection of representative passages. You'll be a better person for having read the book.

As for John A. Saxon, I don't know who the hell he was. Ace didn't publish the Bellem-ghosted book, and Saxon didn't write any others in the genre.

D-89. *Turn Left for Murder.* Marlowe, Stephen (pseud. Milton Lesser). First edition (1955). 142 pp. Hubin, p. 281.

This was the second of three original Marlowe mysteries published as one-half of an Ace Double, none of which featured the author's primary character, the private eye, Chester Drum, a Mike Hammerish hero who pursued espionage and counterespionage missions as much as general detection activities. It was also the second crime novel written by the science fiction writer, Milton Lesser, as Stephen Marlowe.

Lesser's pseudonymous crime-writing career soon outdistanced his science fiction writing and, with other pseudonyms such as Adam Chase, Andrew Frazer, Jason Ridgway, C.H. Thames and one novel as Ellery Queen, he has now written more than forty crime and/or espionage novels.

*   *   *

Death Watch. Wilson, Ruth & Alexander. First paperback edition (1955). 178 pp. Published earlier by Simon & Schuster (1941) as *The Town Is Full of Rumors*. Hubin, p. 441.

"Boss Caine was just back from exile—and already one member of his old political gang was dead! The cops called the death of Caine's former money man a suicide, but the hardened city reporters knew different.

"Arthur Beele, star reporter for the opposition daily, had been around long enough to know most of the unpublishable secrets of Boss Caine's ruthless rule over the city graft. So when he was ordered by his publisher to write the full foul story, he also knew that he was setting up a DEATH WATCH that might include himself."

Isn't it cute how the blurb-writer for this book worked in the title? Isn't the use of the word, "different," in the first paragraph ungrammatical? Aren't I smart for mentioning those things?

This was the authors' only published crime novel.

D-101. *Knock 'Em Dead.* Karney, Jack. First edition (1955). 186 pp. Hubin, p. 231.

Karney wrote eleven crime novels over the course of his career. *Knock 'Em Dead* was about the fight racket. This was the first of two Karney novels to be published as an Ace Double.

• • •

Point of No Escape. Colton, Mel (pseud. Hal Braham). First edition (1955). 134 pp. Hubin, p. 91.

Using the pseudonyms Mel Colton and Merrill Trask, Hal Braham had six original crime novels published during the fifties, four of which were Ace Doubles. *Point of No Escape* was the last.

I've already said more than enough about Colton.

D-109. *I See Red.* Noel, Sterling. First edition (1955). 166 pp. Hubin, p. 307.

Although the author wrote eleven crime-related novels, *I See Red* was the only one published by Ace Books.

I once owned a used copy of another of Noel's novels, *I Killed Stalin,* which I had picked up, as a kid, in Kay's Bookstore, a second-hand book shop in my home town of Cleveland, Ohio. The establishment's clientele also included the young Harlan Ellison who had some roots in the Cleveland area. The book had Harlan's bookplate in it, so he had evidently traded it for some other reading material as we all did in those days.

Several years ago, Harlan learned that I had the book, and, in a nostalgic moment of weakness, called me from California to request its return. Being an altruist, I agreed, especially when he stooped to bribing me with a copy of one of his own books, or did I extort a book from him? I forget.

* * *

Mambo to Murder. Clark, Dale (pseud. Ronal Kayser). First edition (1955). 153 pp. Hubin, p. 83.

The author had this to say about himself back in 1955:

"This is my fourth mystery suspense novel. I finished it between sessions of sitting as a juror in Federal Court. Matter of fact, I'm one of the few jurors (or mystery yarn writers) ever to have solved a real life police case. That was the Cabrillo Freeway Skeleton thing a few years back, and it wasn't brilliant deduction, just leg-work on the scene. Matter of further fact, I got into detective fiction after a period of investigative work in Chicago—four novels and about four hundred magazine stories ago."

Clark had three more crime novels to his credit after *Mambo for Murder,* one of them being *A Run for the Money,* which was his second and last novel published as an Ace Double in 1956.

D-115. Shady Lady. Adams, Cleve F. First edition (1955). 185 pp. See Pronzini & Muller, *1001 Midnights* p. 7-8; Hubin, p. 2.

The author, a contemporary of Raymond Chandler and Cornell Woolrich, began writing for the pulps around 1934, primarily contributing to *Detective Fiction Weekly,* but was also represented in such other pulps as *Black Mask, Detective Tales, Double Detective* and *Argosy.* He turned to novels at the end of the thirties, and most of his work was published during the early forties. Although his career paralleled Chandler, Adams never achieved the stature in the field that Chandler did.

Shady Lady was Adams' last and, arguably, his best work. Shortly after Christmas 1949, Adams died following a heart attack. Robert Leslie Bellem and W.T. Ballard, friends from his pulp-writing days, finished the novel for Adams' widow. An earlier version, *Too Fair to Die,* appeared in *Two Complete Detective Books* for March 1951. The more polished version was published by Ace Books.

There was a prior collaborative effort with Robert Leslie Bellem. *The Vice Czar Murders* (Funk & Wagnalls, 1941) was co-authored with Bellem, with Adams using the pseudonym, Franklin Charles. Bellem also expanded *No Wings on a Cop* (Quin, 1950), another posthumous publication.

Adams' primary series character, Rex McBride, was, in many respects, an anti-hero. The antithesis of the private detective who displayed a tough exterior, but was inwardly sentimental, such as Philip Marlowe and Lew Archer, McBride had a deceptive outward demeanor which concealed a brutal, cynical and hypocritical core and debunked the Chandlerean heroic image of the private eye.

* * *

One Got Away. Whittington, Harry. First edition (1955). 135 pp. Hubin, p. 436.

"He was worth a million dollars to our enemies for the stolen knowledge that he held. He was Gorsucki, runaway scientist. U.S. agent Dan Campbell had finally cornered him and should have had him in handcuffs. Instead, Gorsucki was dead.

"And that made Dan *It* in the eyes of the Bureau—a renegade who'd sold his birthright. They didn't arrest Dan right away because they hoped he'd lead them to the rest of the gang. And Dan knew, even as he ran, that he had to do exactly that—even though the trail was blind, and every clue cold."

D-123. *The Squeeze*.   Brewer, Gil.   First edition (1955). 131 pp. Hubin, p. 48.

The Squeeze is the only Brewer novel published as an Ace Double, as most of his thirty crime novels were published by Fawcett Gold Medal as originals.

Brewer also wrote a number of short stories, some of which appeared in the pulp, *Detective Tales,* in its waning days, but most in the popular digest-sized magazines that succeeded the pulps, such as *Manhunt, Accused, Trapped, Guilty, The Saint, Mike Shayne Mystery Magazine,* and *Alfred Hitchcock's Mystery Magazine.*

Brewer's first novel, *13 French Street,* was published in 1951, as were his earliest short stories in the crime field.

*   *   *

Love Me to Death.   Diamond, Frank.   First edition (1955). 189 pp. Hubin, p. 119.

Love Me to Death was the first of the author's two crime novels published as Ace Doubles, the second being *The Widow Maker* in 1961.

The author's only other two crime novels were published by Mystery House in the mid-forties and featured Ransome Dragoon and Vicky Gaines as their heroes.

D-129. *The Dangling Carrot.* Keene, Day. First edition (1955). 149 pp. Hubin, p. 234.

"Tom Harper left home one morning—and was never seen again. Sam Langley stepped out one evening—and vanished forever. Both prominent in Clay City, neither had ever been involved in scandal or crime. It threw the town into panic, the police into clueless, motiveless confusion.

"To Judge Evan Johns, however, it wasn't quite as interesting as his new election to a higher court. Young for the bench, he figured that for him mysteries must wait until the police themselves dragged the culprits before him for trial. For Evan had decided to celebrate his advancement with the first extra-marital affair of his life—a date with a blonde.

"But at the very moment that the two were secretly shacked up at the lake, the case burst wide open—with the ghastly evidence piled at the very door of Evan's isolated cabin. And then the judge knew that he himself had been picked as a means of getting away with murder."

The Dangling Carrot was the third of the four Day Keene novels published as Ace Doubles.

* * *

Silenced Witnesses. Rosenthal, Norman C. First edition (1955). 169 pp. Hubin, p. 354.

'I'll give it to you straight. Lay off this thing! If you're smart you can take a walk down to the bank someday and find you got a little nest egg you didn't know you had. Say as much as ten grand, maybe more....'

"That's a big chunk of dough and Sol Plato was a cop who could use it. After all, what was there about a routine accident investigation worth the bother? The girl who'd begged him to look into it had changed her mind. The witnesses had all suddenly been struck dumb. Because Plato was an honest cop, he said No.

"But when he woke up the next morning, he found he'd acquired the bribe money anyway!"

Silenced Witnesses was the author's only crime novel.
I should be so lucky as Plato.

D-135. ***Maid for Murder.*** Ozaki, Milton K. First edition (1955).
141 pp. Hubin, p. 316

Ozaki also wrote as Robert O. Saber, penning an even
dozen crime novels under his real name, two of which appeared as Ace Doubles, and a baker's dozen as Saber, none
of which were published by Ace.

The primary publisher under both names was Graphic,
an imprint of Graphic Publishing Co., Inc., a purveyor of original paperback novels during the fifties.

Maid for Murder got some attention from Bill Pronzini in
Son of Gun in Cheek for some dialogue characterized as "The
category of Startling Transformations of Nouns into Verbs":

"What the hell is this all about?" Hara demanded. "Damnit,
I thought I made it clear that you weren't to do any private
dicking!"

Pronzini also pointed out a sex-scene as an example of
an unintentional portrayal of ribald humor:

"She urged me closer, the invitation plainer than if en-
graved on vellum. I grinned, released her hand, and leaned
toward her. Her arms circled my neck and drew me down. A
moment later hot, wire-tinged lips were giving me the kind
of kiss which makes hair sprout on bald-headed men. I leaned
into it, enjoying the surge of unexpected wattage."

I managed to find a few interesting similes such as:

"She reacted by lifting her head and giving me a look as
empty as a bottle on Sunday morning."

"She looked at me with eyes which were as communica-
tive as a pair of bottle caps."

"She was sitting on the edge of the bed, eyes staring from
a thin white face like two brown buttons floating on a puff
of whipped cream."

"The way she was twitching her lips and her hips, she'd
absorb sex like a Kansas farm soaking up rain."

• • •

Dead Ringer. Chase, James Hadley (pseud. Rene Brabazon Raymond). First U.S. edition (1955). 177 pp. Published earlier in U.K. by Hale (1954) as *Safer Dead*. Hubin, pp. 77-78.

Chase, a British writer, wrote more than eighty novels, most of which had American characters and settings. Oddly, he only made a few trips to the United States, preferring to get his local color from encyclopedias, maps and dictionaries of American slang.

Dead Ringer was the only Chase novel published as an Ace Double.

D-147. *My Private Hangman.* Herries, Norman. First edition (1956). 149 pp. Hubin, p. 202.

The author had but two crime novels published, both by Ace Books. *My Private Hangman* was the only one which appeared as an Ace Double. The other, *Death Has Two Faces,* was published in 1955 as a single paperback original bearing the code number S-97.

• • •

Prowl Cop. Jones, Gregory. First edition (1956). 171 pp. Hubin, p. 229.

"She was young and beautiful and blonde. She lay on her back on the rose-beige living-room rug, half naked and seemingly half dead. A bullet hole above one bare breast bubbled red froth as she breathed. An inch higher, another welled crimson in a steady dark stream. A wet spreading stain on the white half slip showed that a third bullet had entered low in the abdominal wall. Her eyes were closed and her breath came and went with a rattling sigh."

Not a bad opening paragraph for the only crime novel published by the author.

D-149. *A Run for the Money.*   Clark, Dale (pseud. Ronal Kayser). First edition (1956). 155 pp. Hubin, p. 83.

"The bathroom door swung open, and a cloud of warm vapor billowed out. The girl in the doorway wore nothing but this steamy cloud. Chip had a moment of incredulous wonder. His hands reached. 'Sheila. honey!' She shrieked at him in a strange voice. Her fists mauled his chest. Her bath-glowing body squirmed and ducked. His astounded eyes took her in. He blurted. 'You're not my wife!'"

Didn't this guy ever see a naked lady before? And to mistake her for his wife, yet. It should only happen to me. Afterwards.

A Run For the Money was the author's second and Final Ace Double.

*   *   *

The Thin Edge of Mania. Macklin, Mark. First edition (1956). 165 pp. Hubin, p. 276

CAST OF CHARACTERS

SUSAN SOL

She eloped with the grim reaper himself!

ELK BOONE

To complete a homicide picture, he needed two models —one alive, one dead.

DANE AIRY

Her slogan was look, talk, but don't handle the merchandise.

MIKE SORETTA

He paid a terrible price for neglecting his daughter's doings.

RAOUL HUSSMAN

Satan was the best customer of his photo studio.

SANDRA WILLS

She had a yen for danger and her hound had a taste for man-meat.

The author must have used up his quota of characters in this book, as it was his only venture into the crime genre.

D-157. *Never Say No to a Killer.* Gant, Jonathan (pseud. Clifton Adams). First edition (1956). 148 pp. Hubin, p. 161.

The author wrote a total of five crime novels, two as by Jonathan Gant. This novel was the only one published as an Ace Double.

* * *

Stab in the Dark. Trimble, Louis. First edition (1956). 171 pp. Hubin, p.408.

The author wrote more than sixty science fiction, mystery and western books during the span of his career, his best being in the western genre. *Stab in the Dark* was the first of eleven crime novels published in the Ace line, although he had a prior novel published in 1953 under his pseudonym of Stuart Brock. (See D-23.)

D-167. *Never Say Die.* Ozaki, Milton K. First edition (1956). 138 pp. Hubin, p. 316.

This was the second and last Ozaki novel to be published as an Ace Double, the first being *Maid for Murder* (See D-135), which received some special attention from Bill Pronzini in *Son of Gun in Cheek.*

I picked out an interesting simile in the prior novel that Pronzini had overlooked, which Ozaki must have liked so much that he used it again. Compare:

"We both drank again and I could feel my body absorbing the liquor like a Kansas farm soaking up rain." *Never Say Die* and "The way she was twitching her lips and her hips, she'd absorb sex like a Kansas farm soaking up rain. *Maid for Murder*

*   *   *

Destroying Angel. Creighton, John (pseud. Joseph Chadwick).
First edition (1956). 181 pp. Hubin, p. 101.

Destroying Angel was the first of eight Ace Doubles
that the author had published between 1956 and 1961. It
was his only output in the crime genre under this
pseudonym. As Joseph Chadwick, he had one other crime
novel published in 1955.

The author has produced over 600 short stories and
novelettes, one motion picture, and nearly two dozen
books outside the genre.

D-170. *Flight by Night.* Keene, Day. First edition (1956). 174 pp.
Published later in U.K. by Red Seal (1960). Hubin, p. 234.

"Bush pilot Jim Bishop was going to face a firing squad
as a convicted murderer at dawn. But now it was the 'hour
for love,' when the banana republic's officials permitted
even prisoners their erotic moments of bliss. And a
beautiful and fiery young woman—a complete stranger—
was led into his cell, offering things beyond his wildest
hopes."

Flight by Night was the last of the four Ace Doubles
written by Keene. He had fifteen more original paperback
novels published before his death by such paperback
houses as Avon, Pyramid, Fawcett and Dell. Although his
primary detective pulp appearances were in *Detective Tales*
and *Dime Mystery,* he also regularly appeared in *Ten
Detective Aces, New Detective, Famous Detective, Smashing
Detective and 15 Story Detective.*

*   *   *

Black Fire. Goldman, Lawrence. First edition (1956). 146 pp. Hubin, p. 171.

This was the author's first crime novel and was followed by seven others, including two novelizations in 1968 of the popular TV series *Judd for the Defense.* At least one original novel, however, *The Heart Merchants,* either marginally qualifies as within the genre or was unconfirmed by Allen Hubin in his research.

D-177. ***The Girl in the Cop's Pocket.*** Turner, Robert. First edition (1956). 157 pp. Hubin, p. 410.

"Will Dennison, a clever mystery writer, concocted a cunningly original method of murder. But that bit of plot threatened to be his own burial ground. For on a visit to his home town, Will found the girl he had once loved accused of killing her husband. And the way the guy got it was straight out of Will's story!"

This novel was the author's second of two that were published as Ace Doubles. As Mercer B. Cook, he wrote one novel in the genre, *In Hot Blood,* published by Challenge (1966). According to Hubin, the book was suppressed, and there are only six known copies. That, of course, would make the book one of the rarest in the world. If you're a Mercer B. Cook completist, however, you've got to have it.

•   •   •

Violence Is Golden. Thames, C.H. (pseud. Stephen Marlowe which in turn is the pseudonym of Milton Lesser). First paperback edition (1956). 163 pp. Published earlier by Bouregy (1956). Hubin, p. 400.

Violence Is Golden was the first of two crime novels written by Marlowe né Lesser under the C.H. Thames pseudonym. The second, *Blood of My Brother,* was published by Permabooks (1963).

D-185. *The Humming Box.* Whittington, Harry. First edition (1956). 155 pp. Hubin, p.436.

"She could not pull her gaze from the man on the floor. He was dead, he had to be dead. She had just shot him only a moment ago, smoke still writhed in a sluggish halo above her head.

"She looked at the gun in her hand, and then realized with a sense of shock that she was still holding the small oblong box, too. Her face twisted and revulsion shook her. This damned box. This damned empty box. Why do I go on holding it? She stared at it for a moment longer, the wire netting turned back from one corner like lecherous, false eyelashes fluttering in an ironic wink. She threw it from her...."

Not a bad opening from the fast-paced "king" of the paperback original, who also wrote as Ashley Carter, Robert Hart Davis, Tabor Evans, Whit Harrison, Kel Holland, Harriet Kathryn Myers, Blaine Stevens, Clay Stuart, Hondo Wells, Harry White and Hallam Whitney.

*   *   *

Build My Gallows High.   Homes, Geoffrey (pseud. Daniel Mainwaring).   First paperback edition (1956). 164 pp. Published earlier by Morrow (1946). See Pronzini & Muller, *1001 Midnights*, pp. 377-378. Hubin, p. 210.

"Thumping good bloodletter."
—*Saturday Review*
"A speedy affair with enough whodunit to keep readers happy."
—*New York Herald-Tribune*
Build My Gallows High was the last of the thirteen mystery novels written by the author between 1933 and 1946. It so established him in Hollywood where he had been writing "B" movies since 1942 that he wrote nothing but screenplays thereafter. The novel was the basis for the classic crime film, *Out of the Past,* which starred Robert Mitchum and Kirk Douglas. An interesting sidenote relates

to Jane Greer, the female lead opposite Mitchum. Nearly forty years later, in 1984, Greer appeared in *Against All Odds,* the remake of *Out of the Past.* In the second film, she played the mother of the character she had portrayed in the earlier version.

D-189. ***Weep for a Wanton.*** Treat, Lawrence. First edition (1956). 174 pp. Published later in U.K. by Boardman (1957). Hubin, p. 407.

The author, one of the earliest proponents of the "police procedural" novel, had an enormous number of short stories published in addition to his seventeen novels, of which *Weep for a Wanton* was his fourteenth and the second of two that were published as Ace Doubles. The novel features three of his primary characters, Mitch Taylor, the veteran street detective, Jub Freeman, the skilled lab detective, and Homicide Lieutenant Bill Decker.

My copy of this Ace Double is reversed in that the novel appears with the cover of the Stephen Marlowe novel which comprises the other half of the book, and vice versa. I wonder if the entire run was bound that way. I'd be happy to be enlightened by any reader who has bothered to read this notation and has a copy in his own collection.

* * *

Dead on Arrival. Marlowe, Stephen (pseud. Milton Lesser). First edition (1956). 145 pp. Hubin, p. 281.

This is the author's fifth crime novel and the third and last to be published as an Ace Double. The novel immediately preceding this one, *The Second Longest Night,* was the first to feature Chester Drum, the private eye who was cast in the Mike Hammer mold. Drum was the major character in most of the novels appearing with the Marlowe pseudonym.

D-195. *The Quaking Widow.*   Colby, Robert. First edition (1956). 171 pp. Hubin, p. 89.

    The Quaking Widow was the author's first of a total of seventeen paperback original crime novels that were published from 1956 to 1972 by such imprints as Gold Medal, Monarch, Avon, Pyramid and Ace. Ace published three more as part of its D-Double series.

• • •

The Deep End. Dudley, Owen (pseud. Dudley Dean MacGaughy). First edition (1956). 148 pp. Hubin, p. 113.

    The author, who also wrote under the pseudonym of Dudley Dean, had three books published as Ace Doubles, of which *The Deep End* was the first. As Dudley Dean, he had one crime novel published by Gold Medal (1960), titled *Lila My Lovely.*

D-197. *TNT for Two.* Byron, James. First edition (1956). 156 pp. Hubin, p. 61.

    TNT for Two was the author's only crime novel. I suppose that he couldn't think of any more titles as catchy and clever as this one, so he quit.

• • •

Counterfeit Corpse. Findley, Ferguson (pseud. Charles Weiser Frey). First edition (1956). 162 pp. Hubin, p. 145.

    Between 1950 and 1956, Findley had five crime novels published. *Counterfeit Corpse* was the only one published as an Ace Double.

D-203. *Uneasy Lies the Head.* Rohde, William L. First edition (1956). 169 pp. Hubin, p. 352.

Rohde wrote seven crime novels between 1950 and 1957, of which this was the only one published as an Ace Double.

Another book, however, received some attention from Bill Pronzini in *Gun in Cheek. Help Wanted—For Murder,* his first novel, which was published by Gold Medal, headed up the chapter titled "Don't Tell Me You've Got a Heater in Your Girdle, Madam!" The quote was:

"Do you believe that those who live violently rarely die in bed? Is it true that he who takes the sword ends with it?

"You've never given it much thought? I didn't, either, until the day Fate hung a delayed fuse on me and blasted my little world into a thousand pieces."

•   •   •

Cain's Girl Friend. Grote, William. First edition (1956). 151 pp. Hubin, p. 184.

This is the author's only crime novel, and it definitely is not set in the land of Nod on the east of Eden.

D-209. *A Night for Treason.* Jakes, John. First paperback edition (1956). 155 pp. Published earlier by Bouregy (1956). Hubin, p. 223.

John Jakes, although well published in the paperback original field, didn't achieve great success until he wrote the "Kent Family Chronicles" series of historical novels. He published under several pseudonyms, including William Ard, Alan Payne and Jay Scotland.

In addition to the half-dozen or so crime novels that he authored, Jakes was active in the science fiction and western fields. In fact, the only other Ace Double under his name was a western, *Wear a Fast Gun* (D-220). As Alan

Payne, however, one other Ace Double was published in 1958, *This'll Slay You* (D-289).

Jakes' first interest was the science fiction field, but he gave it up due to the unenthusiastic response to his efforts. He's probably best known in the field for his Brak the Barbarians stories, a character roughly modeled from the same clay as Conan, Robert E. Howard's famed creation.

*   *   *

Three Times A Victim. Wallace, F.L. First edition (1956). 164pp. Hubin, p.422.

Three Times A Victim was the first of the author's two crime novels, both of which appeared as Ace Doubles. The second was *Wired For Scandal* (D-357).

D-217. *A Rage to Kill.* Lovell, B.E. First edition (1957). 160 pp. Hubin, p. 262.

"Private investigator Edge Hannegan had sent his partner Danny on a routine mission. But Danny never reported back. His bloody, beaten body lay in an alley, surrounded by garbage—and all the evidence said that it was the work of some thrill-crazed young punks.

"Edge knew he wasn't just hunting down some misunderstood juveniles. These particular adolescents were murderous fiends who would attack anyone who threatened their kicks."

Lovell wrote two crime novels. *A Rage to Kill* was the only one published as an Ace Double. The other was *...And Incidentally, Murder!* which was published by Bouregy (1952).

*   *   *

Downwind. McKnight, Bob. First edition (1957). 159 pp. Hubin, p. 272.

Bob McKnight was one of the stalwart writers for the Ace Double series, having had published no less than eleven original crime novels from 1957 to 1962. *Downwind* was the first and was published when the author was fifty-one years old.

D-221. *You've Bet Your Life.* Ashe, Gordon (pseud. John Creasey). First U.S. paperback edition (1957). 172 pp. Published earlier in U.K. by Long (1956) as *No Need to Die*. Hubin, p. 15.

The Creasey listing in *Twentieth Century Crime and Mystery Writers* (Second edition, 1985) extends from page 210 to page 219. As Gordon Ashe, he wrote fifty-three novels, all of which featured Patrick Dawlish, except two. You guessed it: *You've Bet Your Life* was one of the two. The other was *The Man Who Stayed Alive*, Long (1955).

•　•　•

The Terror Package. Chavis, Robert. First edition (1957). 148 pp. Hubin, p. 78.

This was another one-shot effort by an Ace Double author.

D-225. *Loser by a Head.* Giddings, Harry. First edition (1957). 156 pp.

Would you believe? Here's a book not listed in Hubin. Does that mean it doesn't exist? Don't be silly; I'm looking at a copy right now.

•　•　•

A Lonely Walk. Chaber, M.E. (pseud. Kendell Foster Crossen). First
U.S. paperback edition (1957). 164 pp. Published earlier in U.S. by
Holt (1956) and in U.K. by Boardman (1957). Hubin, p. 74.

Crossen wrote twenty-one novels as M.E. Chaber, all
of which featured Milo March, an investigator for the
Intercontinental Insurance Company and sometime CIA
agent. Consequently, March's adventures were roughly
divided into two general categories, the traditional tough
private detective novel and the espionage novel.

Virtually all that Crossen wrote was formula fiction,
which is understandable given his background in the pulps.
As Richard Foster, he wrote a series of novelettes for
Double Detective featuring the Green Lama. The concept
for the character arose early in 1939 when Crossen was an
editor for the Frank A. Munsey Company's *Detective
Fiction Weekly.* He was asked by the head of the magazine
department to work out a character to compete with The
Shadow. The Green Lama was the result: an American who
had gone to Tibet and studied with the lamas, eventually
becoming a lama himself. Upon his return to this country,
he utilized his training to combat evil in the hero pulp
tradition. While The Green Lama never did achieve the
popularity of The Shadow, sales were good. Crossen
continued to write all of the Green Lama stories until
Popular Publications bought out Munsey, and Harry Steeger
dropped *Double Detective* from the Popular line.

D-231. ***Murder for Charity.***   Dudley, Owen (pseud. Dudley
Dean McGauphy). First edition (1957). 158 pp. Hubin, p. 128.

This novel is the second of three published by the
author as Ace Doubles. The cast of characters includes a
working girl named Edith Amen: "Her body was public
property; her heart she gave only once." Guess what kind
of work she did. Hint: She did not operate a municipal
parking garage.

• • •

Point of Peril. Ronns, Edward (pseud. Edward S. Aarons). First
U.S. paperback edition (1957). 162 pp. Published earlier in U.S. by
Bouregy and Curl (1956) and later in U.K. by Red Seal (1960). Also
reprinted as by Aarons by Macfadden (1965). Hubin, p. 353.

Ronns, aka Aarons, like many of the writers whose
careers spanned the decades from the thirties on, wrote for
the pulps. Nearly all of his pulp writing was published
under the Ronns pseudonym, and his work appeared in
magazines such as *Clues, The Phantom Detective, The
Shadow, Detective Story Magazine,* and *Doc Savage.*

Although Aarons wrote three mystery novels in the
thirties and another three in the forties, his career took off
in the paperback originals boom of the fifties. The
"Assignment" series featuring Sam Durrell was his most
successful creation, and a total of forty books appeared in
the series, all being published under Fawcett's Gold Medal
imprint.

Point of Peril was the only Ace Double published
under either of the author's pseudonyms.

D-235. *The Lady and the Snake.* Farr, John (pseud. Jack Webb).
First edition (1957). 149 pp. Hubin, p. 141.

You may now rest easy with the knowledge that the
Jack Webb who appeared as Joe Friday in the popular TV
series, *Dragnet,* is not the same Jack Webb who authored
a number of books featuring Jewish Detective-Sergeant
Sammy Golden and Father Joseph Shanley, a Roman Catho-
lic priest. You may think I'm dumb, but I was never sure
about that until I checked it out because I wanted to tell
the reader something about this book.

The Lady and the Snake, together with another novel
under the John Farr pseudonym, *Don't Feed the Animals,*
have zoo backgrounds. Albert J. Menendez, in *The Subject
Is Murder* (Garland, 1986), categorized other Webb novels
under his somewhat esoteric chapter headings, i.e. the

Shanley/Golden combination in the category of "Holy Terror: Ecclesiastical Murders," and another novel, *The Brass Halo* (Rinehart, 1957), under the "Gardening" heading. He evidently ignored the zoo motif in his book. Is that cruelty to animals, or what?

*   *   *

Nothing to Lose But My Life.   Trimble, Louis. First edition (1957). 169 pp. Hubin, p. 408.

I still can't figure out why Trimble isn't listed in *Twentieth-Century Crime and Mystery Writers*. After all, he wrote nearly thirty novels in the genre under his own name and his two pseudonyms, Stuart Brock and Gerry Travis.

He is, however, listed in *Twentieth-Century Science-Fiction Writers* and *Twentieth Century Western Writers*, even though he probably didn't write as many in either genre as he did in the mystery field. Perhaps it's because he is more highly regarded for his westerns, and he isn't closely associated with mysteries in the average fan's mind, or evidently in the average expert's mind, for that matter.

In any event, this is the second of the many crime novels authored by Trimble in the Ace Doubles series.

D-241. *The Hired Target.*   Tucker, Wilson. First edition (1957). 174 pp. Hubin, p. 409.

Tucker wrote a baker's dozen of crime novels, of which *The Hired Target* was the only one to be published as an Ace Mystery Double. Hubin, however, mistakenly lists Tucker's science fiction novel, *To the Tombaugh Station* (Ace, 1960), in his crime bibliography, possibly because of the mystery/thriller element often used by Tucker in his science fiction novels. Like Louis Trimble, however, he has been omitted from *Twentieth-Century Crime and Mystery Writers*. Again, the explanation might be that he is more widely known for his science fiction writing, and he does appear in *Twentieth-Century Science-Fiction Writers*, but come on. Writers like Trimble and Tucker need to be recognized not only for their contributions to their primary fields, but also in the mystery genre. It's not as if they shot their loads on one mystery and then departed for greener pastures.

If John M. Reilly, editor of the second edition of *Twentieth-Century Crime and Mystery Writers* reads this, I hope that he takes this as constructive criticism for a possible third edition. Writers like Trimble and Tucker should be included. I think I'll get off my soap box now.

*   *   *

One Deadly Dawn. Whittington, Harry. First edition (1957). 146 pp. Hubin, p. 436.

"As Public Relations Director for Twenty Grand Studios, Sam Howell knew that movie stars would do anything for a front-page write-up. So when Jack Roland got himself charged with murdering a scandal magazine publisher, Sam just groaned. It was so obviously a press-agent's stunt.

"Only one thing didn't fit. The police were buying it, lock. stock and barrel. And then it suddenly hit Sam that as much as he knew about the antics of filmland, he was a novice to the vicious racket of the newsstand scandal-mongers. There were too many influential people who didn't want the dead publisher's confidential files aired. It was no longer a question of innocence or guilt; it was simply a matter of hushing the crime up quickly."

D-247. *Not So Evil As Eve.* Creighton, John (pseud. Joseph Chadwick). First edition (1957). 151 pp. Hubin, p. 101.

This novel is the second of eight Ace Doubles published under the Creighton pseudonym, which was his total output in the genre as Creighton.

In addition to the one crime novel published under his true name, he had six crime novels published by Monarch from 1959 to 1961 under the pseudonym of John Conway: *Hell Is My Destination* (1959), *Madigan's Women* (1959), *Requiem for a Chaser* (1960), *This Dark Desire* (1960), *Love In Suburbia* (1961), *Sin In Time* (1961).

* * *

Look Out Behind You.   Lewis, Ken. First edition (1957). 168 pp. Hubin, p. 255.

Another one and only published as an Ace Double. I wonder where Don Wollheim, as editor-in-chief, got these from. Over the transom or under the door? I didn't have the opportunity to ask him before his death.

D-253. The Buried Motive.   Cassiday, Bruce. First edition (1957). 169 pp. Hubin, p. 73.

"Sometimes it's a very short flight indeed for a stool pigeon. One slip of the lip and he's a dead bird.

"Bonding investigator Cash Madigan found that out when he went to Gotham, Missouri, to track down Royal Blaine, an informer who had tipped him off to an embezzler's whereabouts. It was all neat and well-timed, but Blaine's murder foiled the plot and landed Madigan in jail on suspicion of being the killer. Madigan didn't have an alibi, but a beautiful little rich girl came by and unblushingly provided one so good that Madigan wished it were true!

"But all it did was to turn Madigan free to be a pigeon himself...a clay one."

Cassiday wrote six mysteries under his own name of which this was the first of three to be published as an Ace Double.

* * *

Marked Down for Murder. Dean, Spencer (pseud. Prentice Winchell). First U.S. paperback edition (1957). 149 pp. Published earlier in U.S. by Doubleday (1956) and in U.K. by Boardman (1957). Hubin, p. 113.

"Fast-paced with sufficient spice of sex, violence and mystery..."
—*San Francisco Argonaut*
"One of Dean's smoothest and strongest jobs of writing. His best to date."
—*New York Times*
There were nine novels published under the Dean pseudonym, all featuring Don Cadee, a department store detective. *Marked Down for Murder* was the only one published as an Ace Double.

D-259. *The Case of the Violent Virgin.* Avallone, Michael. First edition (1957). 127 pp. Later published in U.K. by W.H. Allen (1960). See Pronzini and Muller, *1001 Midnights,* pp. 29-30; Pronzini, *Gun in Cheek* (1982), pp. 62-64; Pronzini, *Son of Gun in Cheek* (1987), pp. 169-188. Hubin, pp. 17-18.

* * *

The Case of the Bouncing Betty. Avallone, Michael. First paperback edition (1957). 161 pp. Published earlier as "The Bouncing Betty" in the short-lived (2 issues), bedsheet-sized, Avallone-edited magazine, *Private Investigator* (1956) and published later in U.K. by W.H. Allen (1959). See Pronzini and Muller, *1001 Midnights* pp. 29-30; Pronzini, *Gun in Cheek* (1982), p. 62; *Son of Gun in Cheek* (1987), pp. 169-188. Hubin, pp. 17-18.

So what if Opal Trace "musicales," "carols," and "husks" instead of speaking. So what if *The Case of the Violent Virgin* has a plot that is a surrealistic cross between *The Maltese Falcon* and *Murder on the Orient Express.* So what if Avallone has been trashed by Bill Pronzini and the

Noonologist, Francis M. Nevins, Jr. in various genre-related
books. So what! So what! So what! I happen to like Avo.

We first met at Pulpcon in Cherry Hill, New Jersey,
some years ago, where we attempted to clean out the top
shelf of the hotel bar and nearly succeeded. At the same
Pulpcon, we took part in a recreation of an old Doc
Savage radio show, in which I portrayed Doc, in somewhat
campy fashion, and Mike played Miguel, the henchman of
the evil villain, The Feathered Serpent, reading his lines
with an odd accent that bordered on that of a Bulgarian
immigrant in Peru. As I recall, Mike's death throes and
utterings were an astonishing thing to witness.

Okay, so Mike's two hundred plus novels, of which
more than thirty feature Ed Noon, aren't exactly poetry.
And his numerous short stories, one of which even
appeared in *Weird Tales* in the September 1953 issue, may
not measure up to Edgar Allan Poe. But, hell, let's face it.
No one reads Avallone to get an education in American
literature. He is, however, an integral part of American
popular culture and, for me, reading an Ed Noon novel is
as enjoyable as watching a Disney cartoon.

"Noonisms," as some of his more incoherent, but
colorful, phraseology have been dubbed, may abound in
his oddly plotted novels, as do bizarre metaphors and
similes by the score, but who cares? Not I. That's part of
the fun. And every once in a while, one can come across
a passage such as the following, which definitely does *not*
require an apology:

"The Mainliner's wheels hummed, sang and rumbled
through the brisk daylight now. Bright green countryside
flashed by the broken windows. And Opal Trace's
blanket-covered corpse jogged easily and weirdly on the
sill, still half-in, still half-out of Drawing Room B.

"With the stealthy sounds in the corridor, I couldn't
wait any longer. I handed Duffy my .45, stepped over to
the sill and gently eased Opal's body from its awful, almost
disgraceful position. She was heavy. Very heavy in death.
I wrapped the blanket around her more securely and

propped her up against the cushions. I tried not to look at the ugly, drying red splashes on the blanket but they were there all the same. Sitting across from me, Dean's face turned slightly green in shade and he averted his head. His soft profile was still undefined like dough, but now it was puckered and lined a little. Even he had had some feeling about Opal Trace." (The Case of the Violent Virgin.)

I've devoted a lot of time and space to Mike Avallone, and he sure doesn't need me to stave off his critics; he's pretty outspoken on the subject. However, the fact remains that he maintains an uncanny popularity among the Menckenesque "Great Unwashed," and, for that reason alone, deserves a spot in the archives of mystery fiction. As for me, where can I find some more Ed Noon novels?

D-265. *Shooting Star.* Bloch, Robert. First edition (1958). 159 pp. Hubin, pp. 37-38.

∗　∗　∗

Terror in the Night and Other Stories. Bloch, Robert. First edition (1958). 129 pp. Hubin, pp. 37-38.

Contents:
Terror in the Night
Water's Edge
The Real Bad Friend
A Good Imagination
Man with a Hobby
Luck Is No Lady
String of Pearls

God, I love Robert Bloch. Not only is he one of the nicest people in the world, but he's one of the finest writers. At age 75 and still going strong, he has been writing for more than fifty-five years since his first short story sale to *Weird Tales* when he was seventeen.

Shooting Star, a private eye novel set in Hollywood, was published just before *Psycho,* considered by some to be Bloch's magnum opus, saw print and was the second of two Bloch novels published as Ace Doubles, the first being *Spiderweb* (D-59).

Terror in the Night and Other Stories, the flip side of this Ace Double, has the distinction of being Bloch's second published collection of short stories. The Blochophile will, of course, recall that *The Opener of the Way,* Bloch's first collection, was published by Arkham House (1945) and marked Bloch's initial appearance in book form. The book is now a collector's item, fetching a handsome price if one can lay hands on a decent copy.

I saw Bob at DeepSouthCon in Huntsville, Alabama in June 1987, where he was one of the guests of honor. The convention, that year, was sort of a miniature World Fantasy Convention, with such writers in attendance as Hugh Cave, Ramsey Campbell, Charles Grant, Dennis Etchison and Karl Edward Wagner. I had gone at the last minute, as I wanted to see Hugh and Peggy Cave and publicize the Cave collection that I had compiled and edited, *The Corpse Maker* (Starmont, 1988). We thought that the collection would be appearing soon, as well as Audrey Parente's biography of Cave, *Pulpman's Odyssey* (Starmont, 1988), for which Bob Bloch had written an introduction. Neither book was published until July 1988.

Following the convention, I took a shuttle to the Huntsville airport to catch a flight to Memphis where I would change planes and eventually get to Cleveland. Bob Bloch, as Guest of Honor, got VIP treatment. He was driven to the airport by two of the convention gofers in a fancy, expensive sports car. In fact, he was taken by a route that enabled him to see some of the local highlights. The problem was that he couldn't see very well, having recently suffered from some severe eye problems which incapacitated him for most of the weekend. In addition, the sight-seeing tour got the driver somewhat lost, so they didn't arrive at the airport until after Bob's seat to Los Angeles via Atlanta had been given away. Fortunately, an alternate flight plan was arranged which re-routed Bob through Memphis at a cost roughly approximating the national debt. Bob was somewhat upset. One might even say that he was enraged, and it takes a lot to do that.

The gofers left him fuming at the gate and hightailed it away from the vicinity where Bob Bloch's colorful pejoratives were polluting the atmosphere around him at a record clip. Then they saw me coming, told me what had happened and begged me to try to ameliorate the situation, a task which would certainly be no more difficult than parting the Red Sea. Well, I accompanied Bob onto the plane, which was the same flight that I was taking, deboarded with him in Memphis, and stayed and chatted with him until his flight boarded for Los Angeles, about a half-hour before mine left. There actually was no harm done, as the flight that Bob took arrived at about the same time as the original flight, and Bob's wife, who was meeting his plane at LAX, had been alerted about the change.

It wouldn't surprise me to see the perpetrators of that real-life fiasco killed off rather sadistically in one of Bob's future yarns, if his mood at the time was any indication. After all, an incident in Paris provided the basis for one of Bob's eerie stories in which a Fagin-like character suffered irreversible damage at the hands of the protagonist, who had cause to avenge a wrong that had been done him by some street urchins.

D-273. *Shakedown Hotel.* Fredericks, Ernest Jason. First edition (1958). 147 pp. Later published in U.K. by Hale (1959) as *Lost Friday*. Hubin, p. 157.

Shakedown Hotel was the first of two novels published by the author as part of the Ace Doubles line, the second being *Cry Flood!* (D-370).

The two novels published by Ace were the author's only contributions to the genre.

* * *

The Midnight Eye. Roscoe, Mike (joint pseud. John Roscoe and Michael Ruso). First edition (1958). 172 pp. Hubin, p. 354. See Pronzini & Muller, *1001 Midnights*, pp. 696-97.

The authors were real life private detectives, operatives for Hargrave's Detective Agency in Kansas City. They wrote five books together, all featuring the tough Kansas City private eye, Johnny April, who surfaced following the success of Mickey Spillane's Mike Hammer.

The Midnight Eye was the the only one published as half of an Ace Double, and the last in the series, following *Death Is a Round Black Ball* and *Riddle Me This* (Crown, 1952), *Slice of Hell* (Crown, 1954), and *One Tear for My Grave* (Crown, 1955).

D-279. *Bye Bye, Baby!* Bond, J. Harvey (pseud. Russell Robert Winterbotham). First edition (1958). 149 pp. Hubin, p. 40.

Russ Winterbotham had his first science fiction novel, *The Space Egg,* published by Avalon in 1958, the same year that *Bye Bye, Baby!,* his first crime novel, was published as a paperback original. Avalon was the publisher of a line of uniformly packaged hardcovers designed primarily for the library market. Prior to the publication of his novels in 1958, Winterbotham had authored some sixty Big Little Books.

This novel was the first of four genre novels written as J. Harvey Bond, all of which were published as Ace Doubles between 1958 and 1961. Using the same pseudonym, he wrote one science fiction novel, *The Other World,* published by Mayflower (1964).

Mike Lanson, a police reporter, was featured in all of the crime-related novels.

* * *

Murder Mutuel. McKnight, Bob. First edition (1958). 139 pp. See Menendez, *The Subject Is Murder* (1986), p. 234. Hubin, p. 272.

"In a saddle, Joe Trunk was a good jockey. On his feet, he was a heel. But after being dragged halfway around the track by a horse, he was just a very dead little man.

"As a fellow trainer at the Killen Stables, Pat Hover's interest in finding Joe's killer was merely routine. But when suspicion pointed to his own boss, Holm Killen himself, it became a more personal matter. Finally, as the workings of a clever racing 'fix' came to light, Pat found himself up against a desperate struggle to survive against both police suspicion and murderer violence."

This was the second of eleven mystery novels written by McKnight, all of which were one half of an Ace Double.

D-285. ***The Brass Shroud.*** Cassiday, Bruce. First edition (1958). 177 pp. Hubin, p. 73.

This novel was the second of three published as an Ace Double, out of six crime novels written by the author under his own name.

Other crime novels appeared under the pseudonyms of Carson Bingham, Mary Anne Drew, Annie Laurie McMurdie, and Michael Stratford and were published by a variety of imprints such as Monarch, Avon and Lancer.

* * *

Odd Woman Out. Linklater, Joseph (pseud. Alex Watkins). First paperback edition (1958). 143 pp. Published earlier in U.S. by Bouregy & Curl (1956) and later in U.K. by Ward (1959). Hubin, p. 257.

All of the author's seven novels under this pseudonym featured Silas Booth, a private eye in Los Angeles. This is one of a few with this byline; the others were as by J. Lane Linklater. *Odd Woman Out* was the only one of the series to be published as an Ace Double.

Other novels were: *Black Opal* (Mill, 1947); *Shadow for a Lady* (Mill, 1947); *And She Had a Little Knife* (Mill, 1948); *The Bishop's Cap* (Mill, 1948); *A Tisket. a Casket* (Mystery House, 1959); *The Green Glove* (Mystery House, 1960).

D-289. *This'll Slay You.* Payne, Alan (pseud. John Jakes). First edition (1958). 149 pp. Hubin, p. 321.

John Jakes also wrote as William Ard and Jay Scotland, as well as this one-shot crime novel as Alan Payne. This book features Larry Shock and his obese partner, Mr. Moon, in a murder plot involving gamblers and race horse doping.

* * *

Violent City. Hawkins, John and Ward. First U.S. paperback edition (1958). 139 pp. Published earlier in U.S. by Dodd, Mead (1957) and in U.K. by Eyre (1958). Hubin, p. 197.

"Westbury, Wash., described as a 'cow-country Gomorrah,' is the scene of *Violent City*, a yarn tailored to the *Saturday Evening Post* pattern and capably done....It's a perfectly good pattern, including lots of action and told in a pleasantly direct way."
—*San Francisco Chronicle*
This is the only novel by the Hawkins duo to be published as an Ace Double. Between 1944 and 1958, they had seven novels published in hardcover, most of which thereafter enjoyed being reprinted in paperback.

D-297. *The Cut of the Whip.* Rabe, Peter. First edition (1958). 133 pp. Hubin, p.336. Also see Pronzini & Muller, *1001 Midnights* pp. 660-61.

Fawcett Gold Medal published most of Rabe's paperback originals, including his first three books which were published in consecutive months during 1955. Somehow *The Cut of the Whip* managed to sneak in as half of an Ace Double. Like many of Rabe's contemporaries, he wrote espionage novels as well as crime fiction.

One of Rabe's series characters, Daniel Port, is a retired mobster and is featured in *Dig My Grave Deed* (1956), *The Out Is Death* (1957), *It's My Funeral* (1957), *Bring Me Another Corpse* (1959), and *Time Enough To Die* (1959), as well as *The Cut of the Whip.*

* * *

Kill One. Kill Two. Kelston, Robert H. First edition (1958). 154 pp. Hubin, p. 235.

"Until the night he killed a peon with his car, the American engineer had been the hero of Monterrey...and the two most luscious babes in town had been his for the asking. But when it turned out that corpse wasn't that of a common peasant, but that of the notorious husband of one of his two flames, he knew that the death was no accident.

"Whoever had pushed that man in front of his speeding car wanted McCoy available to pay the penalty.

"And when McCoy tried to clear himself, he found that he was slated to play the star role in the famed 'Mexican Sack Game'—all tied up in a bag with the killers and the politicos using him for a football."

This is the second of two genre novels by the author, and the only one published as an Ace Double. His other novel was *Murder's End* (Graphic, 1956).

D-301. *Murder Isn't Funny.* Bond, J. Harvey (pseud. Russell Robert Winterbotham). First edition (1958). 137 pp. Published later in U.K. by Digit (1958). Hubin, p. 40.

Murder Isn't Funny, a murder novel set among the strange world of comic strip writers and artists, was the second of four to be published as part of the Ace Double line, as well as being the only four novels to be published in the genre under the Bond pseudonym.

*   *   *

The Deadly Combo.   Farr, John (pseud. Jack Webb).   First edition (1958). 117 pp. Hubin, p. 141.

The Deadly Combo is the second of two Ace Doubles published under Jack Webb's primary pseudonym. The first was *The Lady and the Snake* (D-235).

Good cover on this one if you like nude women semi-immersed in a tub with, as Ed Noon might say, breasts proudly floating like twin buoys in an apple-bobbing contest. One of the best things about the book, however, is its setting in the world of jazz music.

Webb also had a number of short stories published in many digest magazines of the fifties and sixties, such as *Manhunt, Menace, Alfred Hitchcock's Mystery·Magazine* , and *Accused.*

D-305. *Cornered.*   King, Louis.   First edition (1958). 136 pp. Hubin, p. 239.

"A turn-coat cop is a dangerous man—especially when he gets pushed into a tight corner. In Steve Grogan's case, he had quit the force because he wanted to keep his little girl's life from being endangered. But at heart he was still the kind of cop who wouldn't take a beating lying down.

"Henderson, racketeer chief on the run, needed Grogan's help to make perfect his getaway—and he knew that the best way to get at Grogan was through his daughter. But Grogan didn't need Henderson any way except dead."

The one and only crime novel by this author.

* * *

Free-Lance Murder. Rodell, Vic. First paperback edition (1958) (Abridged). 120 pp. Published earlier by Thomas Bouregy (1957). Hubin, P. 351.

Another one and only genre novel, the difference being that *Free-Lance Murder* somehow managed to get published before Ace reprinted it in its double line.

D-313. *Design for Dying.* Krasney, Samuel A. First edition (1958). 147 pp. Hubin, pp. 242-243.

"'A financial jungle where the fittest create industrial giants and all the rest suck at the udder of someone else's cow. Three hundred thousand people working between 35th and 40th Streets and between Broadway and Ninth Avenue, stealing designs and ideas, cutting each other's throats.'

"That's New York's Garment District. And Homicide Lieutenant Abraham Lincoln Larson found himself in the middle of this teeming labyrinth—between a murderer who kept killing but couldn't be caught, and his chief who wanted Abe off the force almost as much as he wanted a murderer."

Design for Dying was the second of the author's four novels to be published between 1955 and 1963 (and the only Ace Double) to feature Lt. Abe Larson, a homicide dick in New York's tough garment district. It was also the first of Krasney's four crime novels to be published as an Ace Double.

* * *

The Deadly Boodle. Flynn, J.M.   First edition (1958). 109 pp.
Hubin, p. 150.

This is the first of nine novels that were published as
half of an Ace Double between 1958 and 1962 under the
author's J.M. Flynn byline. He had six other crime novels
published by other imprints under the byline of Jay Flynn.

In addition to the nine Ace Doubles, J.M. Flynn did
Surfside 6 (Dell, 1962), a novelization of the popular TV
series of the day, and an unabridged version of *Terror
Tournament* (Mystery House, 1959).

D-317. ***The Big Bite.***   Travis, Gerry (pseud. Louis Trimble). First
paperback edition (1958). 140 pp. Published earlier by Thomas
Bouregy (1957). Hubin, p. 407.

Louis Trimble had three crime novels published under
the Travis byline, *The Big Bite* being the only one put out
as part of an Ace Double. Other books as by Gerry Travis
were *A Lovely Mask for Murder* (Mystery House, 1956) and
Tarnished Love (Phoenix, 1942), the latter only marginally
qualifying, if at all, as a genre novel.

*   *   *

The Wayward Blonde.   Creighton, John (pseud. Joseph
Chadwick).   First edition (1958). 116 pp. Hubin, p. 101.

"'We want those oil maps, Dave.'"
"'I haven't got them, I tell you!'"
"'You're forgetting that we've got your wife, and that
Max is just itching to get his hands on her.'"
"'Frank, I can't take it any more. I'm going to the
police.'"
"'Go to the cops. They'll find your wife for you—but
only when she won't be much use to you.'"
What dialogue! Doesn't it make you wonder who Max
is, and why Frank is holding Dave's wife prisoner until she
gets her period?

D-321. *The Smell of Trouble.* Trimble, Louis. First edition (1958). 121 pp. Hubin, p. 408.

If there are any Louis Trimble collectors out there who are completists, were you aware that he had two stories published in *Detective Yarns,* the pulp that proudly provided "a dozen stories for a dime"? You might want to look for "I've Got a City Full of Sin" (April 1939) and "You Can't Kill a Cadaver" (March 1940). Beware, however. Those issues will cost you a bit more than a dime now.

* * *

Trial by Perjury. Creighton, John (pseud. Joseph Chadwick). First edition (1958). 135 pp. Hubin, p. 101.

This is the fourth of eight books published in the Ace Double line under the Creighton byline.

I have a beautiful copy of this double. Although it's not pristine, the pages are white and crisp, and the spine's in great shape. Many Ace Doubles have browning, brittle pages and tend to fall apart when one tries to read them. So, how do I manage to read my copies if they're in poor condition? That's easy to answer. Very carefully.

D-329. *Stamped for Death.* McDowell, Emmett. First edition (1958). 135 pp. Hubin, p. 269.

* * *

Three For the Gallows. McDowell, Emmett. First edition (1958). 121 pp. Hubin, p. 269.

> Contents:
> All She Wants Is Money
> Set-Up For Murder
> Blood Feud

Stamped For Death was the author's second published novel to appear in the Ace Double line. It was the first to feature the series character, Jonathan Knox, a Louisville,

Kentucky auctioneer with a bad reputation. Sub-dubbed "The Case of the Cancelled Philatelist," it doesn't take a genius to figure out what this mystery is all about.

Three For the Gallows contains three novelettes, all of which feature Knox and are also set in Louisville, Kentucky where the author resided.

D-333. *Scream Street.*   Brett, Mike (pseud. Leslie Frederick Brett). First edition (1959). 125 pp. Published later in U.K. by Digit (1960). Hubin, p.48.

Mike Brett shouldn't be confused with Michael Brett (pseudonym of Miles Barton Tripp), whose series of ten paperback originals featuring private eye Pete McGrath were published by Pocket Books during the sixties.

This Mike Brett, on the other hand, had only two crime novels published, both as Ace Doubles and both featuring Sam Dakkers, whose "head was as bald as the eight-ball he found himself behind."

*   *   *

Stranglehold.   Creighton, John (pseud. Joseph Chadwick). First edition (1959). 131 pp. Hubin, p. 101.

Numero cinco (For those readers who are not multi-lingual as I obviously am, that means number five) of the eight Ace Double originals written by Creighton.

D-347. *The Corpse without a Country.*   Trimble, Louis. First edition (1959). 132 pp. Hubin, p. 400.

"The first time insurance claims investigator Peter Durham's friend Arne Rasmussen had a fire on one of his ships, Peter treated it as a routine accident. The second fire he called bad luck. But when the third fire broke out, Peter knew there was no jinx, but just a very clever arsonist."

Some clever arsonist. No one would ever suspect arson where an insured has three fires and three insurance claims, all within one month. And that's some clever insurance claims investigator to figure it out so quickly.

I've often wondered why people commit arson. They always seem to get caught and go to jail. Insurance companies invariably suspect fraud when a claim is made against a fire insurance policy. On the other hand, how do you start a flood?

                •   •   •

Play For Keeps. Whittington, Harry. First U.S. paperback edition (1959). Abridged. 124 pp. Published earlier by Abelard (1957). Hubin, p. 436.

"Good."
—*Washington Post*

I suppose that abridged review refers to the unabridged edition. I hate abridgements. They always seem to cut the guts out of the original book, although the editor might say that it's just some fat being trimmed to create a lean, mean look.

I'd rather unclog my arteries some other way.

D-349. *The Guilty Bystander.* Brett, Mike (pseud. Leslie Frederick Brett). First edition (1959). 123 pp. Published later in U.K. by Digit (1960). Hubin, p. 48.

This novel, the second of only two written by the author, was also the second to be published in the Ace Double line. As with the first, it featured Sam Dakkers, the bald bookie, who described himself as "sort of a poor man's Yul Brynner."

* * *

Kill Me with Kindness.   Bond, J. Harvey (pseud. Russell Robert Winterbotham). First edition (1959). 133 pp. Published later in U.K. by Digit (1960). Hubin, 40.

"While Mike Lanson, reporter for the *Gazette,* was checking up on Clarence Proost, director of the Anti-Vice League, Proost was slain. There was a strip-tease dancer named Luzy who thought that `maybe' she murdered him. The police thought so too, but Mike didn't so he helped her hide out, hoping for the bigger story to break.

"All the gangsters in town didn't care who killed whom, all they wanted were the blackmail files Luzy had in hiding with her. With everyone on the merry-go-round of murder, Mike knew the odds were high against the real kingpin of crime showing his head—but he was willing to risk his own as well as Luzy's to headline that story."

I'll bet that Luzy was really thrilled to have Mike risking her head for her. After all, she was a sensitive artiste who yearned to have her poetry, not her obituary, published in the *Gazette:*

"Strippers are maidens who are seldom forlorn.
They dance before menfolk the way they were born.
On top of a bar, before lecherous eyes
They bump and they grind for amusement of guys—"

D-357. *Lady in Peril.*   Dent, Lester. First edition (1959). 111 pp. Hubin, p. 260.

Lester Dent was one of the quintessential pulpsters who were able to knock out reams of wordage to satisfy the ever-demanding pulp magazine market. As Kenneth Robeson, he wrote about two hundred Doc Savage novels and contributed numerous short stories during the thirties to such magazines as *Top-Notch, Scotland Yard, Detective-Dragnet, Ten Detective Aces,* and *Crime Busters.*

Possibly his finest work were the two stories that he sold to *Black Mask,* "Sail" and "Angelfish," which have become recognized as classics of the hard-boiled school of detective fiction.

Lady in Peril was Dent's last novel, published around the time of his death on March 11, 1959, after a writing career that spanned approximately thirty years. It was the second of his novels to be published as an Ace Double, the other being a reprint and not an original.

* * *

Wired for Scandal Wallace, Floyd. First edition (1959). 145 pp. Hubin, p. 422.

This novel is the second and last of the author's contributions to the crime genre, both of which were published in the Ace Double line as originals.

D-361. *Dangerous to Know.* Duff, James P. First edition (1959). 133 pp. Hubin, p. 128.

This is the only original of Duff's to appear as an Ace Double. However, he had three other novels published in the genre during the fifties: *Some Die Young* and *Who Dies There?,* both by Graphic (1956), and *Run From Death* (Mystery House, 1957).

•••

Murder Mistress. Colby, Robert. First edition (1959). 120 pp. Hubin, p. 89.

"Driving to Miami, Scott Daniels paused to rescue a lady in distress. She was in a road house, abandoned by her date, and so Scott offered Valerie a lift. No sooner had they started off, then they spotted the boy friend's car smashed in an accident.

"Valerie begged Scott to save her good name by salvaging her suitcase from the wreck before the cops could find it. But no sooner had he done so, then he learned that instead of being filled with pink unmentionables it was loaded with green negotiables—hundreds of thousands of them!"

Not a bad exchange. I've always preferred green to pink.

This is the second of four Colby novels to be published as an Ace Double and has a nakeder-than-usual girl on the cover, wearing, it would appear, nothing but a gun wrapped around her right trigger finger. Some women will do anything to attract attention.

D-367. *Negative of a Nude.*   Fritch, Charles E.   First edition (1959). 120 pp. Hubin, p. 158.

"Mr. Abernathy and the blonde were being playful. I couldn't tell if the girl were a real blonde, but without a doubt the blonde was a real girl. She was wearing a two-piece bathing suit that barely enclosed her magnificent dimensions.

"I noticed Mr. Abernathy had dimensions, too, mostly around his middle. He had a head composed mostly of skin, white-haired around the fringe area; he was paunchy, knobby-kneed, and he didn't look at all the lover-boy his wife believed him to be.

"It was obvious what Mr. Abernathy saw in the blonde. It was equally obvious what the blonde saw in Mr. Abernathy. The blonde was apparently willing to trade some of what she had for some of what Mr. Abernathy had, so everyone was happy.

"Everyone, that is, except Mrs. Abernathy—who was probably not a blonde."

Not a bad wise-cracking opening for a one-shot crime novelist.

* * *

Till Death Do Us Part. Trimble, Louis. First edition (1959). 136 pp. Hubin, p. 408.

Here's how an old pro, writer of more than fifty novels in the crime, science fiction and western fields, opens:

"I was sitting in the two small rooms that remained of my once plush Mexico City office. I was waiting for Rosanne Norton. I had nothing else to do, so I kept myself busy wishing. First I wished that I could get enough money to go and find Enrico Pachuco. Then I wished that if I did find him, I'd be able to figure out some way of making him admit publicly what he'd done to me. And finally I wished that I'd never taken him in as a partner in the first place."

I don't know about you, but the Fritch one-shot opening grabbed me more.

D-373. ***Scarlet Starlet.*** Warren, Doug. First edition (1959). 129 pp. Hubin, p. 426.

Besides this Ace Double novel, set in Hollywood, the author had only two other books published in the field, both by Pyramid, and both, rather appropriately, novelizations of movies: *Walking Tall* (1973) and *A Case of Rape* (1975).

* * *

The Knave of Diamonds. Karney, Jack. First edition (1959). 127 pp. Hubin, p. 231.

The second of the two Karney crime novels to be published as an Ace Double, and the first of two that featured Jim Breen, the insurance investigator, as a series character. Other originals were published in the fifties by such lines as Popular Library, Pyramid, Berkley and Monarch.

D-379. *Mistress of Horror House.* Woody, William. First edition (1959). 120 pp. Hubin p, 445.

This was the only crime novel that the author had published. The title sounds like a blander version of those lead stories in the horror pulps of the thirties which are so dear to me.

· · ·

Drink with the Dead. Flynn, J.M. First edition (1959). 136 pp. Hubin, p. 150.

This is the second of nine books published in the Ace Double line under this particular byline of the author.

A suspense/murder novel about a bootlegging operation in Northern California, it is considered one of Flynn's best non-series novels.

D-387. *Fare Prey.* Fisher, Laine (pseud. James A. Howard). First edition (1959). 146 pp. Hubin, p. 146.

This novel is the only book by the author to be published as an Ace Double.

Under his true name, James A. Howard, he had eight crime novels published in the late Fifties and early sixties, among which were four that were published by Popular Library and featured Steve Ashe as their common series character.

· · ·

The Bikini Bombshell. McKnight, Bob. First edition (1959). 110 pp. Hubin, p. 272.

"After bailing himself out of revolutionary Cuba, Sam Petrie had to lay low in Florida. Rough and tough Madhouse Manny, operator of a shady Havana gambling casino was after his skin. The day that Eustace, Manny's axman, turned up stateside, Sam knew that his number was just about up.

"But while Sam's eye was turned on Eustace, a beautiful masked bikini-clad babe got the drop on him. He didn't know how she fitted into Manny's murderous game, but when she ordered him to start swimming out into the slashing Gulf waters, he obeyed. This had become one fix he couldn't slip out of. He was caught between a she-devil and the deep blue death."

Is that intriguing, or what?

D-393. *Evil Is the Night.* Creighton, John (pseud. Joseph Chadwick). First edition (1959). 138 pp. Hubin, p. 101.

This novel about the U.S. Border Patrol, wetbacks, rape, and revenge is the sixth of eight published as Ace Doubles under the Creighton byline.

•   •   •

Dictators Die Hard. Levey, Robert A. First paperback edition (1959). Abridged. 118 pp. Published earlier by Thomas Bouregy & Co. (1959). Hubin, p. 254.

The second of two crime books published by the author, the first being *Murder in Lima* (Avon, 1957).

D-401. *I Want Out.* Thomey, Tedd. First edition (1959). 117 pp. Hubin, p. 402.

I Want Out was the only one of the author's four genre novels to be published as an Ace Double.

For the benefit of would-be Thomey collectors, the others were: *And Dream of Evil* (Abelard, 1954), *Killer in*

White (Gold Medal, 1956; Fawcett, London, 1958), and *Flight to Takla-Ma* (Monarch, 1962).

•   •   •

Obit Deferred.   Trimble, Louis.   First edition (1959). 139 pp. Hubin, p. 408.

"Jeff McKeon, investigator for the D.A., had developed a burning hatred for the shyster lawyer Aldon Maury. It seems that Jeff had just about pinned down his charge that Maury was the crime overlord in Puget City when his star witness got 'sick' and 'disappeared' before trial time.

"But now it looked as if he had Maury really sewed up on an embezzlement charge. And Jeff began to sweat— because it had been too easy. Something was fishy.

"So when on the day of trial Jeff ran head on into a couple of hired thugs, he realized that the trap he'd set for the crime king had been neatly turned into a murder trap for Jeff McKeon instead."

No, it's just an ugly rumor that I am the crime overlord in Beachwood, Ohio. And I'm not a shyster, either! Anybody want to try for "ambulance chaser."?

D-409. *Cargo for the Styx.*   Trimble, Louis.   First edition (1959). 116 pp. Hubin, p. 408.

I know that this book is supposed to be about mysteries published as Ace doubles, but Trimble was multi-faceted in that he wrote numerous science fiction and western novels as well. In fact, he is most noted for his work in the westerns.

It shouldn't be overlooked, however, that a number of Trimble's westerns have an element of mystery about them that requires investigative techniques on the part of the heroes. Examples are *The Lonesome Mountains* (Ace, 1974), *Marshal of Sangaree* (Ace, 1968) and *The Man from Colorado* (Ace, 1963).

• • •

Terror Tournament. Flynn, J.M. First paperback edition (1959). 140 pp. Abridged. Published earlier by Thomas Bouregy & Co. (1959). Hubin, p. 150.

The "tournament" in the title refers to a Pro-Am golf tournament. Of the protagonist, Burl Stannard, it was said that "trouble was par for his course." The cover proclaims: "They set a course record—for murder." The blurb begins: "Tommy-guns were their driving irons."

I'm confused. How come this isn't a golf murder mystery? It's not listed in Albert J. Menendez's *The Subject Is Murder.* So much for categorization.

D-415. *Dead Certain.* Sterling, Stewart (pseud. Prentice Winchell). First edition (1960). 107 pp. Hubin, pp. 389-390.

Contents:
Dead Certain
A Grave Matter

• • •

Fire on Fear Street. Sterling, Stewart (pseud. Prentice Winchell). First U.S. paperback edition (1960). 149 pp. Published earlier in U.S. by Lippincott (1958) and in U.K. by Boardman (1959). Hubin, pp. 389-390.

Sterling was yet another carryover from the pulp era, having been published extensively in *Black Mask* as well as a multitude of other detective pulps.

This Ace Double combines adventures of two of his primary series characters, Chief Fire Marshal Ben Pedley in *Fire on Fear Street* and hotel detective Gil Vine in the two novelettes which comprise *Dead Certain.* The former series began in the pulps and carried over into nine novels, three of which were reprinted as Ace Doubles.

Sterling wasn't in the same class as Hammett and Chandler; however, he was prolific in his output and had the unique knack of creating unusual "gimmick" detectives which, of course, was typical of the pulps. Another major series featured department store detective Don Cadee (as by Spencer Dean).

D-419. *A Slice of Death.*   McKnight, Bob. First edition (1960). 102 pp. Hubin, p. 272.

An interesting sidelight about the author is that he was an expert horse racing handicapper and, as he has stated, a "semi-retired horse player." In addition, he has had published over three hundred articles about horse racing, as well as a book on picking the odds, *Straight, Place and Showdown.* He has been described by the editors of *American Turf Monthly,* a leading racing journal, as "one of the top handicappers of the day."

McKnight's track experience and racing knowledge were put to good use in writing *A Slice of Death,* which featured a trouble shooter for a big Florida race track, a scheme involving the fraudulent use of the track's tote board, and murder.

•   •   •

Open Season.   Thielen, Bernard. First paperback edition (1960). 154 pp. Abridged. Published earlier by Thomas Bouregy & Co. (1958). Hubin, p. 401.

Thielen had two crime novels published, both originally by Bouregy in its Mystery House line: the other was *A Charm of Finches* (1959). *Open Season,* however, was the only one reprinted as an Ace Double.

D-425. *Dig Her a Grave.* Kruger, Paul (pseud. Elizabeth Roberta Sebenthal). First edition (1960). 121 pp. Hubin, p. 243.

The author also wrote as Harry Davis and had two novels published by Greenberg under that byline in 1956, *My Brother's Wife* and *Portrait of Rene.*

As Paul Kruger, she had nine other crime novels published during the sixties and early seventies, *Dig Her a Grave* being the only one published as an Ace Double. Of the eight, six were published by Simon & Schuster of which five featured lawyer Phil Kramer: *Weed For Willow Green* (1966), *Weave a Wicked Web* (1967), *If the Shroud Fits* (1969), *The Cold Ones* (1972), and *The Bronze Claws* (1972).

•••

A Half Interest in Murder. Creighton, John (pseud. Joseph Chadwick). First edition (1960). 135 pp. Hubin, p. 101.

"Matt Reber, one of L.A.'s private eyes, had three visitors that afternoon: a trembling business man whose life was threatened, a delectable doll with careless curves, and a gangster with an air gun loaded with a poisoned needle.

"Matt knew that somehow they all went together. But before the puzzle was complete Matt found himself in the middle of a strong-arm stock deal, a TV 'Western' where the badmen used real bullets, and a great big murder mystery.

"And the cops were also putting the puzzle together. The only piece they needed was the murderer—and that's when they picked up Matt!"

This novel is the seventh of eight that were published as Ace Doubles, the author's only output in the genre under this byline.

D-433. *If Hate Could Kill.* Bradley, Jack.   First edition (1960).
136 pp. Hubin, p. 45.

The only crime novel published by this author.

* * *

The Smasher.   Powell, Talmage.   First paperback edition (1960).
120 pp. Published earlier by Macmillan (1959). Hubin, p. 331.

"A plot of revenge with an excellent cast of characters.
A wife calls her husband and tells him someone is trying
to kill her. From miles away the husband speeds home to
find his wife dead and a note saying, 'You owe me the kid,
too.' The search for the killer reveals much the husband
had not known before or was unwilling to admit to
himself. Well-written, skilful handling of complicated plot
and fine suspense, this is above average."
    —*Evansville Press*
"Tensely emotional... solved uniquely."
    —*Chicago Tribune*
Talmage Powell made his first professional sale in 1943
and contributed about 500 more stories to various pulps,
digests and anthologies over the years, most of which were
in the crime field. Many of his earliest were filler stories for
The Shadow. Fillers were those stories that followed the
Shadow novels which comprised the bulk of the magazine.
In addition, he wrote twenty novels, of which *The Smasher*
was the first to be published.

D-439. *Run If You Can.* Dudley, Owen (pseud. Dudley Dean
McGaughy).   First edition (1960). 144 pp. Hubin, p. 128.

The third of three Ace Doubles published under the
Owen Dudley pseudonym.

* * *

The Devil's Punchbowl. Decker, Duane. First edition (1960). 112 pp. Hubin, p. 114.

The author's only crime novel.

D-445. *Bloodline to Murder.* McDowell, Emmett. First edition (1960). 147 pp. Hubin, p. 269.

* * *

In at the Kill. McDowell, Emmett. First edition (1960). 108 pp. Hubin, p. 269.

This Ace Double contains the final two books in the five book series featuring Jonathan Knox, the shady auctioneer and sometime murder investigator. Both are paperback originals.

D-447. *The Hot Chariot.* Flynn, J.M. First edition (1960). 144 pp. Hubin, p. 150.

"The man on the slab had not died easily. The grim-faced man with smouldering eyes of a strange pale brown color studied the body at length, seeing the nose that had been pulped, the fragment of bone showing through the ripped cheek, the compound fractures of both wrists, and the raw hole where a kneecap had been. The autopsy surgeon's report, lying ignored on the crumpled sheet, added such details as five broken ribs, ruptured kidneys, and dislocation of vertebrae in the back. The official cause of death was given as skull fracture."

That's one hell of an opening paragraph, provided that one doesn't read it too soon after eating.

* * *

Kiss the Babe Goodbye.   McKnight, Bob. First edition (1960).
112 pp. Hubin, p.272.

The author, a noted racing handicapper in his day,
used his track knowledge in many of his crime novels,
often featuring race track settings. This is not one of those
novels. This one features Lolita, who may have been a
thoroughbred filly, but only had two legs.

D-451. ***Odds against Linda.***   Ward, Steve. First edition (1960).
107 pp. Hubin, p. 424.

A one-shot crime novel about a guy who had his
newlywed bride and his artificial leg kidnapped at the same
time.
Nice bondage cover for those who like that sort of
thing. I do.

• • •

A Key to the Morgue.   Martin, Robert. First U.S. paperback edition (1960). 149 pp. Published earlier in U.S. by Dodd, Mead & Co.
(1959) and in U.K. by Hale (1960). Hubin, p. 284.

"Fast and violent is the action in Robert Martin's *A Key to
the Morgue.* Jim Bennett, the prying eye, gets caught up in a
whirlwind of dangerous doings when a wealthy friend, while
trying to obtain divorce evidence, is murdered and Bennett's
sweetheart is manhandled by a pair of hired thugs.
"If fast guns, savage fists and unscrupulous wit are your
reading meat, this is your bill of fare."
—*Fresno Bee*
This is the first of two novels published as Ace Doubles
that featured Jim Bennett, a private eye based in Cleveland,
who appeared in a total of eleven novels over a period span-
ning about twenty years. The second was *To Have and to Kill*
(F-111). Martin also wrote for a number of detective pulps in
the forties.

Under the pseudonym, Lee Roberts, Martin featured as his series character, Dr. Clinton Shannon, in several novels.

D-459. *The Hot Diary.* Olmsted, Howard J. First edition (1960). 121 pp. Hubin, p. 312.

The author's only crime novel about a private eye with a mundane insurance claims investigation agency who gets to act licentiously macho when a gorgeous dame drops four hundred bucks on his desk. He cools down when the Syndicate shows up. Hey, was that hard-boiled, or what?

*   *   *

Ring around a Rogue. Flynn, J.M. First edition (1960). 134 pp. Hubin, p. 150.

At the beginning of many novels in the Ace Double line, the primary characters were listed with one-line descriptions, such as:

Jere Deal
"A crackerjack automobile dealer, he was so good that he almost dealt himself out of the game of living."
What a subtle play on words.

Sam Travis
"This misnamed female wanted her own car and didn't care who she ran over to get it."

Now we know what makes Sammy run. Groan. Time to quit for the day. I'll try not to say things like that again, but no promises.

D-463. *Dying Room Only.*   Sterling, Stewart (pseud. Prentice Winchell).   First edition (1960). 86 pp. Hubin, pp. 389-390.

*   *   *

The Body in the Bed.   Sterling, Stewart (pseud. Prentice Winchell). First U.S. paperback edition (1960). 170 pp. Published earlier in U.S. by Lippincott (1959) and in U.K. by Boardman (1960). Hubin, pp. 389-390.

This Ace Double offers novels about two of Sterling's primary series characters: Fire Marshal Ben Pedley in *Dying Room Only* and house detective Gil Vine in *The Body in the Bed.*

The Pedley series began in the pulps and was carried over into a series of nine novels, of which *Dying Rooms Only* was the eighth; it was also the only paperback original in the series.

The Gil Vine series had a large New York hotel as its setting, the fictional Plaza Royal. Not only was Vine featured in novels, but the hotel provided the background for such short stories as "Murder Comes to the Plaza Royal" which appeared in the August 1957 issue of *Mike Shayne Mystery Magazine.*

According to the short bio preceding the Gil Vine novel in this double, Sterling was "one of the originators of the 'specialized' or *modus operandi* school of detective story writers as opposed to the private investigator who has no background in any particular field of criminal activity. His Special Squad stories in *Black Mask* were the first to make use of inside techniques as used by the Loft Squad, the Bomb and Forgery Squad, the Criminal Identification Bureau, and the Stolen Property Bureau of the New York Police Department."

D-469. *Man-Killer.* Powell, Talmage. First edition (1960). 145 pp. Hubin, p. 331.

Man-Killer is the second and last Powell novel to be published as an Ace Double, his first, *The Smasher,* being a reprint of the author's first novel. All told, Powell, who wrote hundreds of detective stories for the pulps and digests of the forties and fifties, had only eight crime novels published under his own name. As Ellery Queen, he wrote four others, two of which featured Tim Corrigan.

Powell's primary series character, however, was private eye Ed Rivers, who appeared in five novels; *The Killer Is Mine* (Pocket Books, 1959), *The Girl's Number Doesn't Answer* (Pocket Books, 1960), *With a Madman Behind Me* (Permabooks, 1961), *Start Screaming Murder* (Permabooks, 1962), and *Corpus Delectable* (Pocket Books, 1964).

*   *   *

Running Scared. McKnight, Bob. First edition (1960). 111 pp. Hubin, p. 272.

"Harlan Jamieson was waiting at the dock for a call from his gorgeous ex-wife. The gal was 'kookie,' but he had a date with her anyway. But when the phone rang on his motor cruiser and he answered, it was an unknown man's voice that spoke:

'I'm doin' you a favor, guy. I called to tell you that Mavis just told the cops you stole her little MG.'

"Before Harlan could figure out what kind of double-cross was being pulled, there were sounds of racing footsteps, and the terrified gasping of a man running for his life. Right behind came the sound of a speeding MG—and then the crack of a rifle! Gurgling dead weight hit the water with a splash.

"The bullet might as well have been aimed at Harlan, for he knew whose MG it had to be. And he also knew that he had suddenly become Public Patsy Number One!"

The seventh of eleven McKnight novels published as Ace Doubles.

D-477. *Love Me and Die.* Trimble, Louis.   First edition (1960). 131 pp. Hubin, p 408.

* * *

The Duchess of Skid Row. Trimble, Louis.   First edition (1960). 124 pp. Hubin, p. 408.

Another pair by this Seattle native, which explains the Pacific Northwest locale of many of his mystery novels such as *The Duchess of Skid Row.* He has also resided in Southern California and neighboring Western states, which shows up in *Love Me and Die.*

D-483. *The Corpse in the Picture Window.* Cassiday, Bruce. First edition (1961). 130 pp. Hubin, p. 73.

The last of the three Ace Doubles by this author.

* * *

If Wishes Were Hearses. Bond, J. Harvey (pseud. Russell Robert Winterbotham).   First edition (1961). 126 pp. Hubin, p. 40.

The last of the four Ace Doubles by the author under this byline, all of which featured Mike Lanson, ace crime reporter for the *Gazette.*

D-489. *Somebody's Walking Over My Grave.* Arthur, Robert. First edition (1961). 140 pp. Hubin, p. 14.

The author's only crime novel.

* * *

Dally with a Deadly Doll. Miles, John (pseud. John Miles Bickham). First edition (1961). 116 pp. Hubin, p. 292.

Jack Bickham, primarily a mainstream and western novelist, wrote four crime novels in addition to this Ace Double, which was his first in the field: *The Night Hunters* (Bobbs, 1973; Hale, 1975), *The Blackmailer* (Bobbs, 1974), *The Silver Bullet Gang* (Bobbs, 1974; Hale, 1976), and *Operation Nightfall,* with Tom Morris (Bobbs, 1975; Souvenir, 1976).

D-499. ***High Heel Homicide.*** Davis, Frederick C. First edition (1961). 77 pp. Magazine version titled "Kill Me, Kate." Hubin, p. 111.

•   •   •

Night Drop. Davis, Frederick C. First U.S. paperback edition (1961). 178 pp. Published earlier in U.S. by Doubleday (1955) and in U.K. by Gollancz (1956). Hubin, p. 111.

These were the final two of the three Davis novels published as Ace Doubles under the author's true name. As Stephen Ransome, he had one book published early in the life of the imprint, *I, the Executioner* (D-7).

High Heel Homicide was the last novel by Frederick C. Davis. All subsequent novels were as by Stephen Ransome.

Davis, who wrote a staggering number of stories for the pulps during a career that spanned 25 years, also authored dozens of Operator No. 5 novels as Curtis Steele. Many of these were reprinted in 1966 by Corinth and are collectors' items, although not nearly as collectible as the original pulps.

D-505. *In a Vanishing Room.*   Colby, Robert.   First edition (1961). 127 pp. Hubin, p. 89.

The author began writing while island-hopping with invasion forces in the South Pacific during World War II. He wrote for about seven years before he sold his first story—to a magazine that promptly folded. Colby's first novel sale was to Ace Books which subsequently led to more sales, of which *In a Vanishing Room* is the third of the four published as Ace Doubles.

* * *

The Surfside Caper.   Trimble, Louis.   First edition (1961). 129 pp. Hubin, p. 408.

Nice cover of a blonde holding a smoking gun in her right hand and wearing a backless, strapless gown cut down to bikini level in the rear and held up God-knows-how by a perky pair of whatchacallums (Thank you, Robert Leslie Bellem). If she takes a deep breath, she's wearing her gown around her waist. It wouldn't matter, since there's an apparently dead guy propped in a corner with his eyes closed.

D-511. *One for the Death House.*   Flynn, J.M.   First edition (1961). 141 pp. Hubin, p. 150.

"Burdis Gannon, a private eye in Peninsula City, made a living handling routine cases—skip-traces, background investigations, that sort of thing. But when his unpopular lawyer pal asked for help, he knew this bit would be different.

"For a rich, young blonde deb had been raped and murdered, and a Navy frogman had all but confessed. And now Burd was asked to prove him innocent. Burd knew that when you take a case off the beaten track, you can only find a trail to trouble.

"Burd also knew that you don't turn down a pal. So he took the case—and he found the trouble. For the cops started giving him the cold shoulder, his creditors froze up on him, and some joker did his best to put Burd on ice permanently."

*   *   *

Drop Dead, Please.   McKnight, Bob.   First edition (1961). 114 pp. Hubin, p. 272.

Another horseracing oriented novel by the author, who was considered to be one of the top handicappers of his day, as well as an Ace Double novelist. This one, naturally enough, is about a handicapper who figures out a foolproof horse betting system that nets him out a hundred thousand a year and the trouble he gets into when the syndicate wants a piece of the action.

D-515. ***Kill Me a Fortune.***   Colby, Robert.   First edition (1961). 106 pp. Hubin, p. 89.

Kill Me a Fortune was the last of four Colby novels published as Ace Doubles, all of which were in the D-Series.

Non-Ace publications were: *The Captain Must Die* (Gold Medal, 1959); *The Deadly Desire* (Gold Medal, 1959); *Make Mine Vengeance* (Avon, 1959); *Secret of the Second Door* (Gold Medal, 1959); *These Lonely, These Dead* (Pyramid, 1959); *Run for the Money* (Avon, 1960); *The Star Trap* (Gold Medal, 1960); *Lament For Julie* (Monarch, 1961); *Beautiful But Bad* (Monarch, 1962); *Kim* (Monarch, 1962); *The Faster She Runs* (Monarch, 1963); *Executive Wife* (Monarch, 1963); *Murder Times Five* (Gold Medal, 1972).

*   *   *

Five Alarm Funeral.   Sterling, Stewart (pseud. Prentice Winchell).
First paperback edition (1961). Abridged. 148 pp. Published earlier
by Putnam (1942). Hubin, pp. 389-90.

> "Mile-a-minute action, blustery characters, unrestrained
> language, absorbing background."
> —*New York Herald-Tribune*

This novel was the last of Sterling's five books published in the Ace Double series. It was the author's first
crime novel and featured Chief Fire Marshal Ben Pedley,
who had been a successful character in pulp stories and
novelettes before appearing in hardcover. Pedley was the
main character in a total of nine novels between 1942 and
1962, nearly all of which were hardcover publications.

F-SERIES

1961-1963

$.40

F-SERIES. 1961-1963. $.40.

F-102. *Never Forget, Never Forgive.*   Fox, Clayton.   First edition (1961). 146 pp. Hubin, p. 154.

The author had two crime novels published, both in the Ace Double F-Series. This was the first of the two and featured a deputy sheriff with the improbable name of Thaddeus Zilch. I mean, let's face it, what kind of a name is Thaddeus?

As the first book in the higher priced F-Series, it had an eye-catching bondage cover and a plot that's reminiscent of a certain Clint Eastwood film.

• • •

The Flying Eye.   McKnight, Bob.   First edition (1961). 109 pp. Hubin, p. 272.

The ninth of eleven Ace Double books by this author who evidently made a career out of writing Ace Doubles when he wasn't handicapping the gee-gees.

F-107. *Scratch a Thief.*   Trinian, John.   First edition (1961). 119 pp. Hubin, p. 408.

Scratch a Thief was the only Ace Double published by this author, who had four others published in the genre, two by Pyramid and two by Muller.

*   *   *

My Pal, the Killer.   Warwick, Chester.   First edition (1961). 137 pp. Hubin, p. 426.

This novel was also the author's only one published as an Ace Double. in fact, it was the author's only crime novel.

F-111. ***The Girl from Las Vegas.***   Flynn, J. M.   First edition (1961). 111 pp. Hubin, p. 150.

The author said this about how he came to write *The Girl from Las Vegas:*
"While working as a reporter I really became aware of the strange things people do. Like burying money under the outhouse floor, or leaving a will that's more like a set of clues for a kid's treasure hunt—that kind of thing. And thus the idea of hiding something in Shannahan's bar was born. After all, where else would a good Irishman hide something?"
· The unlikely thing about this book is its title. I've never heard of anyone actually being *from* Las Vegas. Everyone there is from somewhere else.

*   *   *

To Have and to Kill.   Martin, Robert.   First U.S. paperback edition (1961). Abridged. 144 pp. Expanded from an earlier version in *Dime Detective* (June 1949) titled "A Shroud in Her Trousseau". Published earlier in U.S. by Dodd, Mead (1960) and in U.K. by Hale (1961). Pronzini & Muller, *1001 Midnights* (1986) pp. 562-563. Hubin, p. 284.

According to the front of this book, the South Bend Tribune had this to say: "California is the setting for this story of violence among the playboy-playgirl set." Actually, Cleveland is the setting for this novel featuring Jim Bennett, a Cleveland-based private eye, who had his roots in the pulps of the early forties. The reviewer must have gotten confused by the fact that Lake Erie has beaches too.

To Have and to Kill is the second of two Ace Doubles that reprinted earlier hardcover books featuring Jim Bennett. The character was featured in thirteen stories in *Dime Detective* from March 1945 to November 1950, several of which were revised and expanded into novels in the 1950s and 1960s.

F-115. *The Blonde Cried Murder.* Creighton, John (pseud. Joseph Chadwick). First edition (1961). 122 pp. Hubin, 101.

"If Ed Donovan ever had the world by a string, someone had snipped it clean. His wife had skipped, his private detective agency had slipped and he had just about flipped for the bottle."

What a play on words. The last of eight Ace Doubles that were published by the author under the Creighton byline.

*   *   *

Killing Cousins. Flora, Fletcher. First U.S. paperback edition (1961). 133 pp. Published earlier in U.S. by Macmillan (1960) and in U.K. by Cape (1961). Hubin, p. 150.

Fletcher Flora, like many others, had his roots in the pulps, having had stories published in the early fifties in such magazines as *New Detective, Detective Story, Detective Tales, Dime Detective* and *Fifteen Detective Stories.* By the time that his work began seeing publication, however, the pulps were dying out. His short stories were then published in mystery digests such as *Manhunt, Mike Shayne Mystery Magazine, Alfred Hitchcock's Mystery Magazine* and, of course, the regal *Ellery Queen's Mystery Magazine.*

There were relatively few novels to Flora's credit, his strong point being his shorter tales. *Killing Cousins,* his most successful novel, was one of three to be published in hardcover and won the Macmillan Cock Robin Mystery Award in 1960, the other two being *The Irrepressible Peccadillo* (Macmillan, 1962) and *Hildegarde Withers Makes the Scene* (Random House, 1969), the latter being completed by Flora after Stuart Palmer's death and shortly before his own. His other thirteen mystery novels all appeared as paperback originals.

This novel was the only one of Flora's to be published in the Ace Double line.

F-121. *Sing Me a Murder.*   Nielsen, Helen.   First U.S. paperback edition (1961). 166 pp. Published earlier in U.S. by Morrow (1960) and in U.K. by Gollancz (1961). Pronzini & Muller, *1001 Midnights* (1986), p. 598; Hubin, p. 306.

•   •   •

Woman Missing and Other Stories.   Nielsen, Helen.   First edition (1961). 90 pp. Hubin, p. 306.

Contents:
Woman Missing
Don't Sit Under the Apple Tree
Decision
The Affair Upstairs
Compensation

Helen Nielsen just missed the pulp era, but was extensively published in the mystery digests beginning in the mid-fifties. She was one of the few women to write for male oriented magazines like *Manhunt* and *Mantrap.*

Her only book of short stories, *Woman Missing and Other Stories,* was an Ace original with five stories collected from *Manhunt* and *Alfred Hitchcock's Mystery Magazine* and received praise from Anthony Boucher, who was impressed with her work. Boucher said about *Sing Me a*

Murder: "Substantial as a novel of character in the modern vein of suspense, it is as inventive and deceptive as any strict classic puzzle—a meaty book, opulent with unpredictable pleasures."

Four of the author's later novels featured lawyer Simon Drake, a character she first featured in 1951 in *Gold Coast Nocturne* (Washburn, 1951). The others were: *After Midnight* (Morrow, 1966); *Darkest Hour* (Morrow, 1969); *The Severed Key* (Gollancz, 1973); and *The Brink of Murder* (Gollancz, 1976).

F-125. *The Widow Maker.* Diamond, Frank. First edition (1961). 149 pp. Hubin, p. 119.

"The Hudson's waters are freezing you, Dusty Reagan. They're swirling around you and are going to drown you soon. You've got to fight for your life, Dusty. Pull yourself onto the dock; that's it, slowly, slowly.

"You're not safe yet, Dusty. They say you've killed your brother, carved him into little pieces. They want to fry you in the chair.

"There's a maniac killer loose, Dusty. You've got to find him—even if he turns out to be you!"

The Widow Maker was the second of Diamond's crime novels to be published as an Ace Double. Ironically, of four books he had published in the genre, the first and last were Ace Double originals.

* * *

Deep Six. Flynn, J.M. First edition (1961). 107 pp. Hubin, p. 150. The eighth of nine Ace Doubles published by the author under this byline, all but one of which were originals.

For ten years, Flynn had been a crime reporter for the Portland Express, a background that put him in good stead as a crime novelist.

F-130. *The Screaming Cargo.* Flynn, J.M. First edition (1962). 105 pp. Hubin, p. 150.

Flynn's ninth and last crime novel published as an Ace Double.

Unfortunately, none featured the author's series character, McHugh, who appeared in five novels published by Avon under his Jay Flynn byline: *McHugh* (1959); *Viva McHugh* (1960); *A Body For McHugh* (1960); *It's Murder, McHugh* (1960); and *The Five Faces of Murder* (1962). The series was praised by Art Scott in one of his contributions to Pronzini and Muller's *1001 Midnights.*

*   *   *

The Bullet-Proof Martyr. Howard, James A. First paperback edition (1962). 118 pp. Published earlier by Dutton (1961). Hubin, p. 214.

"James A. Howard deserves a prize for a fine murder story and a blood-chilling portrait of a demagogue. His Paul Kenneth Kane, flag-waving head of a clan of 'kinsmen,' is unspeakably evil; Kane's press agent, a newspaper man who literally has sold his soul to the devil Kane, is a horrifying, sometimes pitiable human complex of cynicism and self-loathing."

—*Chicago Tribune*

The Bullet-Proof Martyr was the only one of Howard's seven crime novels to be published as an Ace Double under his true name. As Laine Fisher, he contributed *Fare Prey* (1959) (D-387) to the line. In the mid 1950s, Popular Library published a four-novel series featuring Steve Ashe.

F-143. *End of a Big Wheel.* Fox, Clayton. First edition (1962). 157 pp. Hubin, p. 154.

The second of: the author's two crime novels, both of which were published as Ace Double originals.

*   *   *

A Stone Around Her Neck. McKnight, Bob. First edition (1962). 99 pp. Hubin, p. 272.

"She was a lovely girl with dark hair and violet eyes and a bathing suit that left little to the imagination. The only trouble was, she was dead. And had been for some time before she was fished out of the Gulf, a cement block tied to her at the end of a rope.

"Private Investigator Nathan Hawk soon amassed more clues than thorns on a rose bush, but none of them pointed the way to the murderer. Hawk followed the maze in bafflement, knowing that at any minute the end of the rope might wind up around his own neck."

Remember Hawk Harrelson, who played major league baseball for a while and quit to try his hand at pro golf? I wonder what made me think of him.

F-155. *A Death at Sea.* White, Lionel. First U.S. paperback edition (1962). 127 pp. Published earlier in U.S. by Dutton (1961) and in U.K. by Boardman (1962). Hubin, p. 435.

•   •   •

The Time of Terror. White, Lionel. First U.S. paperback edition (1962). 128 pp. Abridged by author. Published earlier in U.S. by Dutton (1960) and in U.K. by Boardman (1961). Hubin, p. 435.

"For suspense, drama and violence, *A Death at Sea* is your dish.

"This virile mystery, packed with sex, concerns the explosion of a charter boat and the destruction of six persons aboard. The brother of Eric Carter, skipper, is suspicious and comes to Key West to investigate. He runs into immediate trouble with hoodlums and fringe bad boys.

"The action is fast and the plot is cleverly handled. *A Death at Sea* is good reading."

——*Pensacola News Journal*

"*The Time of Terror* by Lionel White deals with the anatomy of a kidnapping, the story of a kidnapper who finds himself kidnapped.

"The writer skillfully weaves into his terror-laden and suspense-filled story the workings of law enforcement agencies in tracking down the culprits. The author offers a fresh twist to a theme often used before; an amateur bungler finds himself involved with pros after the kidnapping of a child.

"Action, logic and an ending of terror which builds and holds. You can't ask for much more in this kind of fiction."

—*Beverly Hills Times*

The author had this to say about writing for a living: "It's one way to make a living if you are too lazy to work or too incompetent to hold a job."

Nevertheless, he managed to write a number of books, specializing in the "caper" novel, a sub-genre in the mystery field, which deals with the step-by-step planning, execution and aftermath of large-scale crimes.

The two novels published as Ace Doubles and combined in this volume are not indicative of the author's best work either in or out of his caper formula specialty. This Ace Double was somewhat unique in that it was the first to combine two reprint editions.

F-166. *Maigret Has Scruples.* Simenon, Georges. First U.S. paperback edition (1962). 120 pp. Published earlier in France as *Les Scrupules de Maigret* (1958) and as a separate volume in U.K. by H. Hamilton (1959) and as part of the twosome, *Versus Maigret*, by Doubleday (1960) in the U.S. Translated from the French by Robert Eglesfield. Hubin, pp. 374-78.

*   *   *

Maigret and the Reluctant Witnesses. Simenon, Georges. First
U.S. paperback edition (1962). 128 pp. Published earlier in France
as *Maigret et la Temoins Recalcitrants* (1959) and as a separate vol-
ume in the U.K. by H. Hamilton (1959) and as part of the twosome,
Versus Maigret, by Doubleday (1960) in the U.S. Translated by
Daphne Woodward. Hubin, pp. 374-78.

"Simenon was born on Friday, Feb. 13, 1909, in Liege,
Belgium. His superstitious mother registered the birth a day
earlier; the mechanical alteration proved to be anything but
unlucky. Her desire that her son become a baker collapsed
when he learned to read and write at the age of four; at
eleven took a job in a bookshop; then became a reporter
and newspaper columnist.

"With the same directness characteristic of all his work,
at sixteen he wrote a novel in ten days. To Paris, at
nineteen, writing feverishly. In this period he wrote some
200 novels; at one time had six stories, written under
different names, in a single issue of a magazine. He bought
a car, and hired a chauffeur, solely to deliver manuscripts
to the offices of his publishers. At his writing peak, he was
turning out 80 pages each day.

"Not satisfied, at 27, living aboard a sloop, he got
serious about quality, and Maigret was born. Publication
of the first two, in 1930, made the Inspector famous in
France and eighteen other countries within a few months.
Twenty Maigrets appeared in less than two years; to date,
fifty-three."
    —*Roanoke Times*
    Anthony Boucher had this to say in the New York
Times:
    "The Maigret novels of Georges Simenon are always
short—around .50,000 words—though emphatically
'full-length' in plot and in psychological content; and many
years ago they used to appear two-to-the-volume. After a
decade or so of individual books, this generous practice is
now revived....
    "*Maigret Has Scruples* is one of the high points of the
entire Maigret series. Each party to a marriage suspects the

other of mental aberration that may be homicidal; the
problem is one of preventing rather than solving a crime,
and its nature is such that Maigret, that superb intuitive
psychologist, is forced to study the terms and techniques
of clinical psychology. The plot is firm and fascinating; the
characters are real and ambivalent; the telling is direct and
cogent.

"Maigret and the Reluctant Witnesses deals with a
murder during an obviously faked burglary attempt and a
procedural duel between the veteran policeman and a
bright, brash young *juge d'instruction.* The case is an
interesting one, curiously French in its motivation, and the
element of formal puzzle-detection is stronger than usual
in Simenon's work, and very skillfully handled."

The cover of the latter book is unusual in that it
misrepresents the title as *Maigret and the Reluctant Witness.*

F-229. *The Dead and the Deadly*. Trimble, Louis.   First edition
(1963). 120 pp. Hubin, p. 408.

This novel was the author's last crime novel published
in the Ace Mystery Double series. However, Trimble had
a number of others published as Ace Western and Science
Fiction Doubles following *The Dead and the Deadly.*

*   *   *

Homicide Handicap.   McKnight, Bob.   First edition (1963). 102
pp. Hubin, p. 272.

Homicide Handicap was the eleventh and last of
McKnight's novels published as Ace Mystery Doubles, the
only publisher he had. Oddly, the novel, carrying a title
which was apt for a writer who was also an expert
Thoroughbred handicapper, had nothing to do with
horseracing.

G-SERIES

1963

$.50

G-Series. 1963. $.50.

The entire G-Series consisted of books by women authors and, in each case, both sides of the Double were by the same writer. The series was retitled Ace Giant Double Novel Books *and consisted primarily of reprint titles, although several were originals.*

G-501. *The Unsuspected.* Armstrong, Charlotte. First U.S. paperback edition (1963). 159 pp. Published earlier in U.S. by Coward McCann (1946) and in U.K. by Harrap (1947). Hubin, p. 13.

• • •

Incident at a Corner. Armstrong, Charlotte. First U.S. paperback edition (1963). 96 pp. Published earlier in U.S. by Coward, McCann (1959) as one of a pair of novelettes comprising *Duo* and in U.K. by Davies (1960). Hubin, p. 13.

"The festival of Halloween ten days ago was, I trust, celebrated with particularly fitting rites in Glendale, Calif.; for there dwells one of the few authentic spellcasting witches of modern times: Charlotte Armstrong....

"As you may have noticed, I tend to become inarticulate in reviewing Armstrong, largely because the method by which she achieves her magical effects defies critical analysis. You are simply caught up, as you might be by a collaboration of Cornell Woolrich and Shirley Jackson, with all the former's insistent terror of the everyday-gone-wrong and the latter's combination of fantastic imagination and realistic feminine insight."

Anthony Boucher

—*New York Times,* Nov. 10, 1957

The Unsuspected was adapted into a motion picture of the same name by Warner Brothers (1947), starring Claude

Rains, Joan Caulfield, Audrey Totter and Hurd Hatfield. It was directed by Michael Curtiz.

The novel was also suggested by Ellery Queen as one of the 1946 entries in *The Haycraft-Queen Definitive Library of Detective-Crime-Mystery Fiction: Two Centuries of Cornerstones 1748-1948.*

Of *Incident at a Corner,* Anthony Boucher had this to say in his New York Times review: "Charlotte Armstrong, long established mistress of daylit terror-in-ordinary, is in splendid form....Chilling, yet warm, intense yet humorous, meatier and more satisfying than most longer thrillers."

G-503. *The Stairway.* Curtiss, Ursula.   First U.S. paperback edition (1963). 123 pp. Published earlier in U.S. by Dodd, Mead (1957) and in U.K. by Eyre & Spottiswoode (1958). Hubin, p. 106.

*   *   *

The Face of the Tiger.   Curtiss, Ursula. First U.S. paperback edition (1963). 132 pp. Published earlier in U.S. by Dodd, Mead (1958) and in U.K. by Eyre & Spottiswoode (1960). Hubin, p. 106.

"Ursula Curtiss is probably the best contemporary exponent of the 'feminine' mystery, and her insight and economy are often more reminiscent of Elisabeth Sanxay Holding than Mary Roberts Rinehart....Mrs. Curtiss' high professional skill in delicately shifting suspicion and tension builds to a highly ingenious surprise."
—*New York Times*

The Face of the Tiger is considered by many aficionados to be one of the author's best novels among the more than twenty that she wrote.

G-506. *Black Mail* Disney, Doris Miles. First U.S. paperback edition (1963). 147 pp. Published earlier in U.S. by Doubleday (1958) and in U.K. by Foulsham (1960). Hubin, p. 121.

• • •

Did She Fall or Was She Pushed? Disney, Doris Miles. First U.S. paperback edition (1963). 108 pp. Abridged. Published earlier in U.S. by Doubleday (1959) and in U.K. by Hale (1962). Hubin, p. 121.

Many of the author's mystery novels featured three of her ongoing series characters:

Insurance Investigator Jeff DiMarco, who appeared in *Dark Road* (Doubleday, 1946), *Family Skeleton* (Doubleday, 1949), *Straw Man* (Doubleday, 1951), *Trick or Treat* (Doubleday, 1955), *Method in Madness,* (Doubleday, 1957), *Did She Fall or Was She Pushed?,* (Doubleday, 1959), *Find the Woman* (Doubleday, 1962), and *The Chandler Policy* (Putnam, 1971).

Postal Inspector David Madden in *Unappointed Rounds* (Doubleday, 1956), *Black Mail* (Doubleday, 1958), and *Mrs. Meeker's Money* (Doubleday, 1961), all of which were reprinted in the Ace Giant Double Novel Book series.

Connecticut small town policeman Jim O'Neill, who was Disney's earliest creation, appeared in *A Compound for Death* (Doubleday 1943), her first detective novel, *Murder on a Tangent* (Doubleday, 1945), *Appointment at Nine* (Doubleday, 1947), *Fire at Will* (Doubleday, 1950), and *The Last Straw* (Doubleday, 1954).

For what it's worth, Jacques Barzun and Wendell Hertig Taylor, in *A Catalogue of Crime* (Harper & Row, 1971), had this to say about Disney: "Of her more than thirty Crime Club novels, *Compound for Death* (1943) and *The Departure of Mr. Gaudette* (1964) are representative examples, competent without question, but also without distinctive appeal to mind, heart, or sense of style."

G-508. *The Schemers.*   Fenisong, Ruth.   First U.S. paperback (1963). 129 pp. Published earlier in U.S. by Doubleday (1957) and in U.K. as *The Case of the Gloating Landlord* by Foulsham (1958). Hubin, pp. 142-43.

*   *   *

But Not Forgotten.   Fenisong, Ruth.   First U.S. paperback edition (1963). 127 pp. Published earlier in U.S. by Doubleday (1960) and in U.K. as *Sinister Assignment* by Foulsham (1960). Hubin, pp. 142-43.

Of the author's twenty-two crime novels, all of which were published in Doubleday's Crime Club, twelve, in addition to *But Not Forgotten,* featured Lieutenant (later Captain and sometime Acting Inspector) Gridley Nelson of the New York Homicide Department.

I love quoting Barzun and Taylor from their *Catalogue of Crime* (Harper & Row, 1971); they are definitely not sycophantic in their opinions. They say of Fenisong:

"[she] writes stories that conform to the canons of the genre but without that special art of invention and characterization which is needed to lift one murder after another out of the rut."

G-509. *The Innocent Mrs. Duff.*   Holding, Elisabeth Sanxay.   First paperback edition (1963). 147 pp. Published earlier by Simon & Schuster (1946). Hubin, p. 208.

*   *   *

The Virgin Huntress. Holding, Elisabeth Sanxay. First paperback edition (1963). 107 pp. Published earlier by Simon & Schuster
(1951). Hubin, p. 208.

"For my money she's the top suspense writer of them all."
—Raymond Chandler

"Back in the early thirties, before anyone ever heard
of psychological novels of suspense, Elisabeth Sanxay
Holding was writing them, and brilliantly. And she's still the
Old Mistress who can give cards and spades to any of the
Jenny-come-latelies in the field. For subtlety, realistic
conviction, incredible economy, she's in a class by herself."
—Anthony Boucher

Of *The Innocent Mrs. Duff:*

"Packed with hair-trigger action and hard-to-bear
suspense. A beautiful job!"
—Saturday Review

"Filled with surprise and shocks, here is an impressive
suspense novel, a novel so nerve-wracking it will keep you
on the edge of your chair until finished. *The Innocent Mrs.
Duff* is a taut and absorbing drama of a man's slow
disintegration, a luminous and exciting drama of twisted
character...."
—Montgomery Advertiser

Of *The Virgin Huntress:*

"A gem of suspense writing."
—Atlanta Constitution

"Mrs. Holding packs this short book with tense
situations and almost unbearable suspense as she tells the
story of Montford Duchesne, handsome and luxury-loving.
He thinks he has a great future with Dona Luisa, whom he
accidently met in New York the evening of V-J Day.

"Dona Luisa is rich and generous and is fascinated by
Montford because he reminds her of someone she loved
a long time ago. Her niece, Rose, begins digging into
Montford's past because she wants to protect her aunt from
a young man who seems far too mysterious.

"As fast as he tries to cover up, he finds Rose a step ahead of him on his tortuous trail. The struggle between two determined people is destined to end in violence."
—*St. Louis Post-Dispatch*

The author's sometime series character, Lieutenant Levy, appears in neither of the two novels in this Ace Double.

G-511. *Who's Been Sitting in My Chair?* Armstrong, Charlotte. First edition (1963). 95 pp. Hubin, p. 13.

* * *

The Chocolate Cobweb. Armstrong, Charlotte. First U.S. paperback edition (1963). 161 pp. Published earlier in U.S. by Coward McCann (1948) and in U.K. by Davies (1952). Hubin, p. 13.

"He was a young man who worked nights; his name was Johnny Baer. He came home one morning, turned on his light, took one look around his apartment and said, out loud, 'Who's been sitting in my chair?'"

So opens this original paperback novel. The hero quickly discovers the answer to the burning question that first appeared in the suspenseful "Goldilocks and the Three Bears." Evidently, in *this* story, it was a strange lady who previously occupied his apartment and now chooses to sit in it all night. I presume that it's the same golden-locked lady who sits in the chair on the cover of the book. I'm not sure I care.

Of the gothic romance, *The Chocolate Cobweb:*
"....the method by which she achieves her magical effects defies critical analysis."
—Anthony Boucher

"The intricacies of the plot are so skillfully handled that there is no confusion."
—*New York Times*

"Based on the same successful formula as *The*

Unsuspected."
   —*New Yorker*
   "The narrative skill is considerable and the tale a tense performance."
   —*Chicago Sun*

G-512. *The Girl Who Had to Die.*   Holding, Elisabeth Sanxay. First U.S. paperback edition (1963). 101 pp. Published earlier by Dodd Mead (1940). Hubin, p. 208.

                                    •   •   •

The Blank Wall.   Holding, Elisabeth Sanxay. First U.S. paperback edition (1963). 155 pp. Published earlier by Simon & Schuster (1947). Hubin, p. 208.

   Of *The Girl Who Had to Die:*
   "Here's the most important crime novelty in a month of Sundays, so different in approach and execution from the standard brands as to take first place in any list of current offerings. To come right out with the talking points, Mrs. Holding's narrative style is probably foremost, and if you don't think that couldn't help turn a brilliant trick, you haven't sampled *The Girl Who Had to Die*....It is admirably suited to the special kind of shudders, horrid hints, nightmare overtones and general wickedness dealt in by the wicked characters."
   —*New York Herald-Tribune*
   "This is one of those practically perfect jobs that you dream about—and hope for—and look forward to—and read through—and tell your friends about. And then your friends read it and wonder what's wrong with you.
   "Why?
   "Because you've talked. You might have recommended. You shouldn't have discussed.
   "We hereby recommend. And with no discussion. We're tight-mouthed about this one. But we envy you the

experience of reading it for the first time."
—*San Francisco Chronicle*
Of *The Blank Wall:*
"You'll certainly want to know why Mrs. Lucia Holley, a nice housewife, secreted the body of her daughter's nasty suitor in a marsh on Simm's Island....

"Mrs. Holding's mystery critters, indeed, are so freshly drawn as to startle the crime addict, hagridden by mystery types and miscellaneous trash. And that goes even for her lowdowns, especially for Donnelly, a new kind of blackmailer."
—Will Cuppy
New York Herald-Tribune
"Highly recommended."
—*New Yorker*

G-513. *Then Came Two Women.* Armstrong, Charlotte. First edition (1963). 90 pp. Hubin, p. 13.

•   •   •

Catch-as-Catch-Can. Armstrong, Charlotte. Second U.S. paperback edition (1963). 166 pp. Published earlier in U.S. by Coward McCann (1952) [and as *Walk Out on Death* by Pocket Books (1954)] and in U.K. by Davies (1953). Hubin, p. 13.

"Charlotte Armstrong is a major name in American mystery."
—*Los Angeles Daily News*
Of *Catch-as-Catch-Can:*
"Again shows her originality in developing a high pitch of suspense."
—Drexel Drake
Chicago Tribune
"Very stimulating and unusual."
—*New Yorker*

G-518. *The Opening Door.* Reilly, Helen. Second paperback edition (1963). 171 pp. Published earlier by Random House (1944) and Dell (1956). Hubin, pp. 343-44.

*   *   *

Follow Me. Reilly, Helen. First U.S. paperback (1963). 116 pp. Published earlier in U.S. by Random House (1960) and in U.K. by Hale (1961). See Barzun & Taylor, *A Catalogue of Crime,* (1971), p. 356. Hubin, pp. 343-44.

Both mysteries in this Ace Giant Double Novel Book feature Inspector Christopher McKee of the New York Police Department, the author's well known series character, who appeared in nearly all of her police procedural novels. Many of the Inspector McKee plots were based on stories from police files, which she often simplified due to the true facts being too incredible as fictionalized works.

The Opening Door had its genesis as a serial in *The Saturday Evening Post,* while *Follow Me* is described by Barzun & Taylor as "A sophisticated chase from New York to New Mexico, in a legitimate search for needed evidence."

G-519. *The Old Battle Axe.* Holding, Elisabeth Sanxay. First paperback edition (1963). 146 pp. Published earlier by Simon & Schuster (1943). Hubin, p. 208.

*   *   *

The Obstinate Murderer. Holding, Elisabeth Sanxay. First U.S. paperback edition (1963). 109 pp. Published earlier in U.S. by Dodd Mead (1938) and in U.K. by Lane (1939) as *No Harm Intended.* Hubin, p. 208.

Of *The Old Battle Axe:*

"This is for fans who want to be puzzled every step of the way, not just worried about whodunit. Mrs. Holding cooks up plot and yet more plot in a way that should keep readers in a real dither about the demise of Mme. Pascal de Belleforte, formerly Madge Pendleton, of the Long Island Pendletons—if, indeed, the corpse is hers.

"Madge arrived from Paris in a shocking state of disrepair, swallowed two double martinis at a waterfront dive, then got bumped off at the home of her nice sister, Mrs. Herriott, who denied her identity; leaving you faced with question after question and slightly dazed by some of the phenomena of Mystery Land."

—*New York Times*

Of *The Obstinate Murderer:*

"...*The Obstinate Murderer* is decidedly different from the average story of its type. With a beautiful country guest house for background, the author draws the reader into the sinister web of fear and terror which holds the occupants of the house in its grasp. Van Cleef, the detective, becomes one of the central characters in a charming romance which affords him some relief from the horrible chain of events which follows.

"As usual, it is just one little stroke, far too clever, which gives the murderer away, but the mystery connoisseur must be wide-awake to discover it."

—*New Bedford Standard-Times*

G-521. *Mischief.* Armstrong, Charlotte. Second U.S. paperback edition (1963). 123 pp. Published earlier in U.S. by Coward-McCann (1950) and Pocket Book (1951) and in U.K. by Davies (1951). Hubin, p. 13.

*   *   *

The Better to Eat You. Armstrong, Charlotte. Second U.S. paperback edition (1963). 164 pp. Published earlier in U.S. by Coward-McCann (1954) [and as *Murder's Nest* by Pocket Books (1955)] and in U.K. by Davies (1954). Also reprinted in Three-in-One Detective Book Club edition by Walter Black. Hubin, p. 13.

> Of *Mischief:*
> "For sheer, crawling horror, this story beats anything of the kind I have ever read. Not that there are no better horror stories, but I know of none that does so well with simple material and plot, such a commonplace setting and an almost casual, matter-of-fact air."
> —*Chicago Tribune*
> "A fine, chilly combination of terror and suspense."
> —*The New Yorker*
> Of *The Better to Eat You:*
> "An accomplished blending of romance and complex villainy."
> —*The New Yorker*

G-523. *The Forbidden Garden.* Curtiss, Ursula. First U.S. paperback edition (1963). 114 pp. Published earlier in U.S. by Dodd, Mead (1962) and in U.K. by Eyre & Spottiswoode (1963); published later in U.S. as *Whatever Happened to Aunt Alice?* by Ace (1969). Hubin, p. 106.

* * *

Hours to Kill. Curtiss, Ursula. First U.S. paperback edition (1963). 108 pp. Published earlier in U.S. by Dodd, Mead (1961) and in U.K. by Eyres & Spottiswoode (1962). Hubin, p. 106.

> *The Forbidden Garden,* a thriller about a little old lady who had a tendency to plant her hired companions beneath a stand of poplars at the edge of her lawn so that she could cop their nest eggs, proves once again that truth

can follow fiction. Some years ago, there was a little old
lady in California who had a garden full of social security
pensioners who had been her lodgers until she decided to
appropriate their monthly checks.

Part of *Hours to Kill* was published in *The Ladies' Home
Journal* as *Stranger at the Wedding*. Anthony Boucher, in
a New York Times column, said: "An unusually fine
specimen of the imperiled-heroine thriller-romance.... It
managed to startle even this case-hardened reviewer."

G-524. *Who's Afraid?* Holding, Elisabeth Sanxay. Second U.S.
paperback edition (1963). 137 pp. Published earlier by Duell (1940)
and as Bonded Mystery No. 14 (1959). Hubin, p. 208.

*   *   *

Widow's Mite. Holding, Elisabeth Sanxay. First U.S. paperback
edition (1963). 150 pp. Published earlier in U.S. by Simon &
Schuster (1953) and in U.K. by Muller (1954), Hubin, p. 208.

Of *Who's Afraid?*:
"Susie Alban, traveling representative for a cultural
course, was utterly inexperienced in the ways of the world,
and had no idea why the people with whom she came in
contact acted so strangely or why so many of them were
interested in her movements. Gradually, she became aware
that she herself was in danger, but she did not know why
or from what quarter the danger threatened...

"The author has succeeded admirably in depicting the
mounting horror and suspense of the situation in which
Susie, through no fault of her own, had become in
extricably entangled. *Who's Afraid?* does not follow the
usual pattern of the detective story, but it holds the reader's
attention in a way that few books in that category are able
to equal."
—*New York Times*

Of *Widow's Mite,* a mystery featuring Lieutenant Levy, the author's continuing series character in several novels, and Holding's last book before her death on February 7, 1955:

"E.S. Holding was one of the first American writers to bring literary polish to the detective story. She continued to uphold her standards in *Widow's Mite. "*
—*New York Times*

"Quiet horror, crisp dialogue and perceptive character-ization."
—*Columbus Dispatch*

G-525. *The Tentacles.* Leon, Dana. First paperback edition (1963). 149 pp. Published earlier by Harper (1950). Hubin, p. 265.

*   *   *

Spin the Web Tight. Lyon, Dana. First edition (1963). 106 pp. Hubin, p. 265.

Of *The Tentacles:*
"A psychological thriller that holds you from its come-on opening scene to its unexpected and spectacular finish."
—*Book-of-the-Month Club News*

"Dana Lyon writes with a rush of enthusiasm and her scenes are planned with a sure instinct for drama. This is a book for those who want exciting reading with a little more substance than is usually found in the psycho-thriller."
—*New York Times*

Spin the Web Tight was the sequel to *The Tentacles* and was a paperback original. Both novels featured Hilda Trenton.

G-526. *The Dream Walker.* Armstrong, Charlotte. Second paperback edition (1963). 179 pp. Published earlier in U.S. by Coward McCann (1955) and as *Alibi for Murder* by Pocket Books (1956) and in U.K. by Davies (1955). Hubin, p. 13.

* * *

The Mark of the Hand. Armstrong, Charlotte. First edition (1963). 76 pp. Hubin, p. 13.

The Dream Walker "is the story of a plot—a cold, brilliantly calculated plot designed to ruin a man's life. The main characters involved in the plot were only four people, but the cast included hundreds of extras (unwilling, unknowing, but important), and a method of operation so fantastic that even the most suspicious would never question it. All of the plotters had motives: money, power, jealousy and revenge. All were willing to cheat and lie. But only one of the four knew that one element of the plot, the crowning touch, was to be murder."

The Mark of the Hand tells the tale of Betsy Follett, who, when she took a position in the Kilburn household, "thought she had found a piece of Paradise. But she was soon to learn that murder lurked in at least one person's heart. But which one?

"Not the old lady who read mysteries and got about the house with a spryness belying her years....

"Not the handsome Widower who relaxed in the shooting range beneath the house...

"Not the guest who came out of the past with nothing and desired to enter the future with everything...

"Not surely the child, whose trusting eyes and baby mouth did not know the way of a lie...

"Then who? Whose was the hand that left the mark of murder?"

G-528. *Certain Sleep.* Reilly, Helen.   First U.S. paperback edition (1963). 136 pp. Published earlier in U.S. by Random House (1961) and in U.K. by Hale (1962). Hubin, pp. 341-42.

* * *

Ding Dong Bell.   Reilly, Helen.   First U.S. paperback edition (1963). Published earlier in U.S. by Random House (1958) and in U.K. by Hale (1959). Hubin, pp. 341-42.

Both novels featured the author's on-going series character, Inspector Christopher McKee, who appeared in thirty-one of the author's mystery novels, beginning with *The Diamond Feather* in 1930.

The author, who was the mother of Ursula Curtiss, another mystery writer appearing in several Ace Giant Double Novel Books, died shortly after completing *Certain Sleep,* her thirty-fourth novel. She wrote thirty-eight novels in all, of which three appeared under her pseudonym, Kieran Abbey.

G-529. *Mrs. Meeker's Money.* Disney, Doris Miles. First U.S. paperback edition (1963). 138 pp. Published earlier in U.S. by Doubleday (1961) and in U.K. by Hale (1963). Also serialized by the Chicago Tribune Syndicate. Hubin, p. 121.

* * *

Unappointed Rounds. Disney, Doris Miles. First U.S. paperback edition (1963). 148 pp. Published earlier in U.S. by Doubleday (1956) and in the U.K. as *The Post Office Case* by Foulsham (1957). Hubin, p. 121.

Both sides of this Ace Giant Double Novel Book feature Postal Inspector David Madden.

"Mrs. Meeker was not *a* Mrs. Meeker but *the* Mrs. Meeker, seventy-nine and worth about $30,000,000. She'd managed to hold onto most of it, too, until she hired a private detective to trace the grandson of a former lover. Several months and some $50,000 later, she realized she was being swindled and called on Postal Inspector David Madden for help. Neither one suspected that fraud was soon to be mixed with murder!"

Of *Unappointed Rounds:*

"Fast-moving yarn...excellent detective story."

—*Saturday Review*

"Fascinating."

—*New York Times*

"Human and satisfying."

—*San Francisco Chronicle*

G-530. *Net of Cobwebs.*   Holding, Elisabeth Sanxay. First U.S. paperback edition (1963). 118 pp. Published earlier in U.S. by Simon & Schuster (1945) and in U.K. by Corgi (1952). See Pronzini & Muller *1001 Midnights,* p. 374. Hubin, p. 208.

•   •   •

The Unfinished Crime.   Holding, Elisabeth Sanxay. First U.S. paperback edition (1963). 135 pp. Published earlier in U.S. by Dodd, Mead (1935) and in U.K. by Newnes (1936). Hubin, p.208.

Marvin Lachman, who wrote the entry on *Net of Cobwebs* for *1001 Midnights,* stated that it was one of the author's best books, which is exceptional praise considering the high regard in which Holding was held by both Anthony Boucher and Raymond Chandler.

Of *The Unfinished Crime:*

"It is at once different from the ordinary mystery yarn and at the same time holds the rapt attention of the reader."

—*Oakland Tribune*

"Elisabeth Sanxay Holding is noted for the ingenuity of her plots, but in *The Unfinished Crime* she has created a masterpiece of suspense, and shown that committing an unpremeditated murder is like buying an automobile—that

it is not the initial cost, but the upkeep that makes a person pay and pay and pay."
—*New York Sun*

G-531. *Not Me, Inspector.* Reilly, Helen. First U.S. paperback edition (1963). 151 pp. Published earlier in U.S. by Random House (1959) and in U.K. by Hale (1960). Hubin, pp. 341-42.

* * *

The Canvas Dagger. Reilly, Helen. First U.S. paperback edition (1963). Abridged. 135 pp. Published earlier in U.S. by Random House (1956) and in U.K. by Hale (1957). Hubin, pp. 341-42.

About *Not Me. Inspector:*
"A new Helen Reilly novel is always an event, especially when her talented detective, Inspector McKee, must untangle a murder which almost remains unsolved because of a common piece of electrical equipment. In this case, although the victim has supposedly been seen at various times and places during a two weeks period, an autopsy discloses that his last meal had been eaten two weeks ago. So, how could people have seen him?
"We're not going to tell you for it would spoil the plot of the book. We guessed one of the murderers but we certainly failed to guess the accomplice. Excellent as usual."
—*Berkeley Gazette*
About *The Canvas Dagger:*
"'At 4:35 on the afternoon of October third Grant Melville, a portrait painter, fell from the fourth floor studio of the Melville house on East Tenth street and was instantly killed.'
"The verdict was accident. There was one dissenting voice, however, for shortly after four o'clock on that same afternoon, Sarah Casement was standing at a window directly across the street from the Melville house in Greenwich Village when she thought she saw the shadow

of another man standing alongside Melville in his studio. But when she told the police her story, they didn't believe it—until later events brought Inspector McKee of Homicide into the case."

G-533. *The One-Faced Girl.* Armstrong, Charlotte.   First edition (1963). 58 pp. Hubin, p. 13.

* * *

The Black-Eyed Stranger. Armstrong, Charlotte.   Second U.S. paperback edition (1963). 165 pp. Published earlier in U.S. by Coward McCann (1951) and Pocket Book (1952) and in U.K. by Davies (1952). Hubin, p. 13.

The One-Faced Girl, at 58 pages, can only by a stretch of the imagination be considered a novel. Maybe in the mystery pulps or the more recent digests, but, at best, such a length is no more than a novelette. However, it was the fifth and last original Charlotte Armstrong book to be published by Ace, all of which appeared in the Ace Giant Double Novel Book series.

Preceding *The Black-Eyed Stranger* was the following biographical information about the author, whose career spanned nearly thirty years and twenty-eight novels and two short story collections:

"The list of Charlotte Armstrong's novels of mystery and suspense is impressive. Beginning in 1942 with the creation of the detective MacDougall Duff, as in *The Case of the Weird Sisters,* Miss Armstrong hit the jackpot in 1946 with *The Unsuspected.* Outselling all novels of its type in its first year, it was followed in 1948 by *The Chocolate Cobweb,* and in 1950 by *Mischief.* This book established Charlotte Armstrong's leadership position once and for all. Following this came others including *Catch-as-Catch-Can* and the present book."

Armstrong's first collection of short stories, *The Albatross* (Coward McCann, 1957) was Queen's Quorum Number 115.

G-534. *Speak of the Devil.* Holding, Elisabeth Sanxay. Second paperback edition (1963). 129 pp. Published earlier by Duell (1941) and, as *Hostess to Murder* in digest size, by Novel Selections, Inc. (1943) in its Mystery Novel Classics series. Hubin, p. 208.

* * *

Kill Joy. Holding, Elisabeth Sanxay. Second paperback edition (1963). 157 pp. Published earlier by Duell (1942) and, as *Murder Is a Kill-Joy,* by Dell (1946). Hubin, p. 208.

This Ace Giant Double Novel Book was the last of six such publications of holding crime novels in Ace's G-Series, which reprinted a dozen of her eighteen mysteries. *Speak of the Devil* was lauded by the Baltimore Sun as "a thriller of high quality, unusual both in its setting and in the way it is handled. Strongly recommended." *Kill Joy,* likewise, enjoyed favorable reviews as in the San Francisco Chronicle: "Another beautiful study in the subtle and miasmic horror of emotions such as only Mrs. Holding can bring off."

The author, while best known for her mystery novels, also had a total of seven romantic novels published, as well as a number of short stories which appeared during the forties and fifties in such magazines as *Mystery Book Magazine, Ellery Queen's Mystery Magazine, Nero Wolfe Mystery Magazine, The Saint,* and *Alfred Hitchcock's Mystery Magazine.*

G-535. *The Frightened Child.* Lyon, Dana. Second paperback edition (1963). 115 pp. Published earlier by Harper (1948) and, as *House on Telegraph Hill,* by Mercury Mystery (1951). Hubin, p. 265

.

• • •

The Lost One. Lyon, Dana. First U.S. paperback edition (1963). 139 pp. Published earlier in U.S. by Harper (1958) and in U.K. by Gollancz (1958). Hubin, p. 265.

Erle Stanley Gardner reviews *The Frightened Child:*

"*The Frightened Child* is a very fine novel of suspense and it contains an authentically interesting behind-the-scenes glimpse of courtroom psychology and strategy. The author has done a perfectly swell job, and back of that is an interesting development in detective fiction. When lightning keeps on striking in the same place, we know there's a reason."

Charlotte Armstrong reviews *The Lost One:*

"To read *The Lost One* was an excruciating experience. I found myself reaffirming myself in the chair, saying, "Wait, now, don't be so upset. This is just a story!

"The trouble with that is the knowledge that this sort of thing has happened, can happen, may even now be happening.

"The thing that gives me in particular, some pause is this. For the first time, I get some inkling how my own book *Mischief* may have affected the innocent picker up of books from the library. Oh dear....

"Thanks for letting me see it."

Dana Lyon's career spanned more than thirty years, with only eight novels to show for it. Her first, *The Bathtub Murder,* a joint effort with Josephine Hugheston, was published in 1933 and her last, *The Trusting Victim,* was published by Ace in 1964 as a single original paperback. She also had a short story, "The Absent-Minded Professor," published in the June-July 1947 digest-sized issue of *Shadow Mystery,* as well as a number of others in various digest mystery magazines over the years. She was definitely not a prolific writer.

G-539. ***Duet in Death: Composition for Four Hands and The House.*** Lawrence, Hilda (pseud. Hilda Kronmiller).   First paperback edition thus (1963). 121 pp. and 103 pp., respectively. Published earlier in U.S. as *Duet of Death* by Simon & Schuster (1949) and in U.K. by Chapman (1949). *Composition for Four Hands* was reprinted separately by Bestseller (1950) as *Death Has Four Hands* and *The House* was reprinted by Bestseller (1950) as *The Bleeding House.* Hubin, p. 248.

"Miss Lawrence creates horror atmosphere the hard way, with a light touch that leaves no brush marks. The mere suggestion of a sinister sound, the barest hint of screaming silence, and the reader's hackles come away from his collar."
—Meyer Berger
New York Times Book Review
By 1947, Lawrence was being touted by Howard Haycraft as "Far and away the most exciting new talent in the American mystery field today," presumably because of her trio of mystery novels which combined the eccentric investigative group effort of Private Investigator Mark East and spinsters Bessie Petty and Beulah Pond: *Blood upon the Snow* (Simon & Schuster, 1944); *A Time to Die* (Simon & Schuster, 1945); and *Death of a Doll* (Simon & Schuster, 1947).

Although critically acclaimed, she never wrote another novel. The two reprinted novelettes which comprise this Ace Giant Double Novel Book, the penultimate in the series, were her last published longer works.

G-543. ***They Buried a Man.*** Davis, Mildred.   First paperback edition (1963). 129 pp. Published earlier by Simon & Schuster (1953). Hubin, pp. 111-12.

•   •   •

The Dark Place. Davis, Mildred.   First paperback edition (1963).
126 pp. Published earlier by Simon & Schuster (1955). Hubin,
pp. 111-12.

"Mildred Davis won the Mystery Writers of America
Edgar for a best first novel with her *The Room Upstairs,* and
then let five years pass before she followed it with her even
better second, *They Buried a Man.* Her third novel, *The
Dark Place,* cuts the gap between books to two years; and
it's to be ardently hoped that she continue this
diminishing ratio, since she has a welcome and distinctive
talent to bring to the field.

One cannot so far define 'a Mildred Davis novel;' the
three books have been different in subject matter and tone.
But all three have been at once sensitively and solidly
written—subtle in their psychological implications but firm
in their plotting. It's an uncommon combination that may
recall Margaret Millar; and certainly *The Dark Place* is not
unworthy of Millar as study in pure terror."
—Anthony Boucher

*This was the final
Ace Giant Double Novel Book.
R.I.P.*

AUTHOR-TITLE INDEX

AUTHOR-TITLE INDEX

Fox, Clayton
Fredericks, Ernest Jason,
Fritch, Charles E.
Gant, Jonathan
Giddings, Harry
Goldman, Lawrence
Goldthwaite, Eaton K.
Grayson, Charles
Grote, William
Hawkins, John and Ward
Herries, Norman
Hodges, Carl G.
Holding, Elisabeth Sanxay
Homes, Geoffrey

Whittington, Harry

Wilson, Alexander and Ruth

Woody, William

TITLE INDEX

TITLE INDEX

www.ingramcontent.com/pod-product-compliance
Lightning Source LLC
Chambersburg PA
CBHW020245290326
41930CB00038B/395